COUNT THE STARS

A Handbook on Biblical Numbers

STEPHEN C. SHAFFER

COUNT THE STARS

Copyright © 2026 by Stephen C. Shaffer

All rights reserved.

No part of this book may be reproduced in any form or by any electronic or mechanical means, including information storage and retrieval systems, without written permission from the author, except for the use of brief quotations in a book review.

All Scripture quotations, unless otherwise indicated, are taken from the New Revised Standard Version Bible (NRSV), copyright © 1989 National Council of the Churches of Christ in the United States of America. Used by permission. All rights reserved worldwide.

Scripture citations marked (NIV) are taken from the Holy Bible, New International Version, NIV. Copyright ©1973, 1978, 1984, 2011 by Biblica, Inc. Used by permission of Zondervan. All rights reserved worldwide. www.zondervan.com The NIV and New International Version are trademarks registered in the United States Patent and Trademark Office by Biblica, Inc.

    Peniel Press
    43 Stowe Terrace Brantford, ON N3T 6P2 Canada
    www.penielpress.com

Cover design by Olga Shaffer
Cover background image by Brenda Clarke (Texture/Background 11)

PAPERBACK ISBN: 978-1-0688675-1-4
EBOOK ISBN: 978-1-0688675-2-1

*For Mom,
who welcomed a curious child
and his questions
in her bible study*

Contents

Introduction	iii
How to Read the Bible: *An Overview*	1
Haven't I Seen That Somewhere Before?: *Repetition in the Bible*	14
Finding the Center: *Understanding Repeated Numbers*	25
Mourning Into Dancing: *Reversal and Redemption*	39
The Sum is Greater than the Parts: *Combining Numbers in the Bible*	51
Greater Glory: *Comparing Numbers in the Bible*	59
Loaves, Fish, and Baskets: *The Feeding Miracles as a Case Study for Biblical Numbers*	70
Conclusion	83

Introduction

"He took him outside and said, 'Look up at the sky and count the stars—if indeed you can count them.'"

– Genesis 15:5

"Daddy, what does 'avenge' mean?"

I was supposed to be telling my eight-year-old daughter a bedtime story — making up something with kittens, pigs, and unicorns. But then this question popped up.

"Where did you hear that?"

"I was reading through Genesis and I saw that word," she opened her Bible to read, "If Cain was avenged seven times, Lamech seventy-seven times." (She is reading Genesis 4).

It was a beautiful and honest question. I talked with her about revenge and payback and thought about how to tell her that this is not the way of Jesus. Instead of telling, I asked a simple question:

"Where else in the Bible do we hear about something happening seven or seventy-seven times?"

She thought for a few moments. Then her eyes lit up.

"Well, I remember Jesus saying that we should forgive seventy-seven times."

This launched into a short, but powerful, conversation about choosing forgiveness over revenge because we belong to Jesus. This conversation happened for three reasons:

1. She felt comfortable asking a question. She knew she would not be mocked or seen as foolish because she didn't understand something in the Bible. She knew her question was good.

2. I asked a question to make a connection between the confusing passage she was reading and a clearer one where she knew the meaning.

3. She had learned to slow down enough to pay attention to the Bible.

What I experienced with my daughter at bedtime is why I wrote *Count the Stars*. I want to invite you to join me in slowing down and paying attention. I want you to feel comfortable asking questions of the numbers in the Bible. Most of all, I want you to come to the Bible confident that God will meet you there. This book is about the numbers in the Bible, but — more than that — it is a book about how to approach the Bible with anticipation and joy, rather than anxiety and fear. We can grow as readers of the Bible by paying close attention to the way God uses numbers in Scripture.

Learning to Climb a Tree

Imagine you are climbing a tree. As you begin, you reach up to grab a branch above your head. You hang from it slightly, letting it carry some of your weight. If the branch holds firm, then you are confident you can use it to climb higher, because it is strong enough to support you.

However, if it bends significantly, you are likely to look for a different branch for climbing so that it does not break underneath you.

Not every branch of a tree is able to bear the same amount of weight. Thicker branches nearer to the trunk are usually much stronger than the twigs out on the farthest branches. All are part of the tree and all are important, but they are not equally strong. As children (and adults) learn to climb trees, part of growing in wisdom is learning to sense how much weight a given branch is able to carry.

What is true for branches on a tree is also true for interpreting the Bible. We need to learn how much weight an interpretation of a given detail can be made to carry. "All Scripture is God-breathed, and is useful for teaching, reproof, correction, and training in righteousness" (2 Tim. 3:16). Every book and every verse is important and intended to be in the Bible. By the work of the Holy Spirit, the writers were inspired to write as they did, and the scribes and copyists preserved the text as they did. There are no mistakes or accidents in the Bible. We should pay attention to every detail. Jesus himself says, "Not one letter, not a stroke of a letter will pass from the law until all is accomplished" (Mt. 5:18). Jesus took every letter of the Law seriously and we should too.

However, the importance of every detail does not mean that every *interpretation* of those details should be foundational for how we understand God, his work, and his will for our lives. Some ways of understanding the teaching of Scripture are core, essential, and foundational for the Christian faith. To deviate or to depart from them is to leave behind the Christian faith itself. Teachings such as the Trinity, the Deity of Christ, the Two Natures of Christ, the Cross and Resurrection of Christ, and more fall into this category. In church history and theology, these core teachings are often summarized in a "rule of faith"[1] that could be used to evaluate whether we were interpreting the Bible correctly. For instance, if we are reading the Bible and think it says that Jesus is not God, then we are reading it wrong. If we read the Bible and think it says that there is not one God, but three gods, then we are reading it wrong. Whenever Scripture is abundantly clear, we can be confident it can bear our weight.

These core doctrines that must be confessed by all Christians are like the strong central branches of the tree. Whether we are seeking to climb higher and grow as disciples or whether we are seeking to rest in true comfort, these branches can bear our weight. Whenever we are reading and interpreting the Bible and our interpretation lines up with these core teachings, we are on solid footing. We can build a tree house on those branches.

However, not every branch in the tree can bear the same amount of weight. Not every interpretation bears the same amount of weight either. Part of growing in wisdom is understanding how much weight your interpretation of a particular passage can bear.

Why talk about all this at the beginning of a book about interpreting the numbers in the Bible? Let me be clear. I do not believe that every interpretation is of equal value or that we can make Scripture say whatever we want it to mean. I also don't believe that every teaching in the Bible outside of the Apostles Creed is somehow "up for grabs." As we will talk about in the next chapter, I believe the Bible is clear, sufficient, inspired, and authoritative. Yet, the tree analogy

---

[1] Though the "rule of faith" was not always explicitly stated, the ecumenical creeds — The Apostles Creed, the Nicene Creed, and the Athanasian Creed — provide a good summary of the core teachings.

is important because there is a particular temptation for Christians when reading the numbers in the Bible — we can be tempted to try and attach a tire swing to a bunch of twigs.

There are a multitude of books and videos claiming that they have "cracked the code" of the Bible by noting patterns in the numbers, letters, and verses in the Bible. Usually, these come in the form of end times predictions and claims to discovering the "true knowledge" that "they" have been hiding from you all along. We should be suspicious of these types of books for two reasons. First, anyone who claims to have the "secret knowledge" of the real Christianity that has been kept from you is selling you something. There is no secret code in the Bible. In fact, a secret code is the opposite of why the Bible was written. The Bible itself says, "But these are written that you may believe that Jesus is the Messiah, the Son of God, and that by believing you may have life in his name." (John 20:31). A secret code defeats the purpose of trying to let people know about Jesus and believe in him.

Second, the numbers and patterns in the Bible are important and valuable, but they cannot bear the weight that some want to make them bear. In my first handbook on reading the Bible, *The Sinews of Scripture*, I felt the need to argue for the importance of the genealogies in the Bible, because they are often skimmed over by even the most faithful readers. However, when it comes to the numbers in the Bible, I often feel the need to caution in the opposite direction. Do not read more into the numbers than is really there. We will discuss questions and strategies for trying to understand what these numbers mean and why God placed them into the Bible, but this is not some sort of secret code. Rather, this is just the application of the method of reading the Bible where we *pay attention to the details* and *read from a posture of Christian faith*.

NUMBERS IN THE BIBLE

If I have to issue a warning about over-reading these parts of the Bible in the introduction of the book, then why even write a book on biblical numbers? The truth: most people reading the Bible are not sure how to make sense of them. Because all Scripture is God-breathed, we believe they must be important, but we don't know why God felt it was important for us to know that Jesus was in the wilderness for forty days (Mt. 4:2) or why Jesus sent out seventy disciples[2] to declare that the kingdom of God had come near (Luke 10:1-12). We believe these things to be true, but we are not always sure what they mean. This is especially true when we encounter the sizes of armies, the number of descendants, or the measurements of the temple. There are numbers throughout the Bible and many of us feel overwhelmed making sense of them.

Count the Stars is an attempt to help ordinary Christians grow in their confidence when reading the Bible. We will provide tools, questions, and examples for every part of this approach to the biblical numbers. While I hope that you end up agreeing with every interpretation in this book, it is quite possible that you will not be convinced in every case. That is okay. Reading the numbers well adds layers of depth to our understanding of Scripture, but the numbers are not load-bearing branches. Even if you disagree at some points, my hope is that by going through all of them, you will see the overall wisdom of this way of reading the Bible.

---

[2] or seventy-two depending on the translation or manuscript.

Introduction

OUTLINE OF THE BOOK

Count the Stars is divided into seven main chapters, structured around four key questions to ask when encountering numbers in the Bible. Each chapter ends with a series of discussion questions that can be used individually or with a group. The first chapter takes a step back to explain our overall approach to reading the Bible by asking, "What is the Bible?" and "What is it for?" before trying to answer, "How do I read the Bible?"

The second chapter takes an initial look at the four key questions we should ask every time we come across a number in the Bible. Repetition in the Bible is a clue to pay attention and one of the most important strategies for reading the Bible well. This chapter begins the exploration of some frequently repeated numbers in the Bible.

The third chapter explains more deeply what to do when we see a number repeated regularly in the Bible and explores where to find the center of meaning for a particular biblical number.

The fourth chapter looks at what to do when one instance of a biblical number seems to run counter to all the other examples of that number in the Bible.

The fifth chapter discusses the possibility of one number representing a combination of several other key biblical numbers and further examines what that might mean.

While most of the chapters focus on repeated numbers, chapter six looks at when we should compare different numbers in the Bible. When the situation is similar, but the numbers are quite different, this is another clue to pay attention.

In chapter seven, we will try to put together all that we have learned in order to look at the two different feeding miracles of Jesus.

Numbers are everywhere in the Bible. They are not a secret code. They cannot bear the whole weight of your faith. Instead, they are one of the ways that God calls us to pay attention and make connections across the Bible so that we can see more clearly who he is, what he has done, and his call upon our lives. Read correctly, the numbers in the Bible can bring us joy and wonder as we read God's Word.

Discussion Questions:

1. What word would you use to describe how you usually feel when trying to read the Bible? (e.g. do you feel excited? Do you fear not understanding? Do you feel confused? Joyful? Dread? Duty? Delight?)

2. If we think about interpreting the Bible like climbing a tree, where do you often find yourself: going way out on a limb with little fear of falling, arms and legs wrapped around the trunk and unwilling to step out on any branch, or still on the ground so afraid of falling it is hard to start climbing?

3. How might it change your faith to able to approach the Bible confident that God will meet you and nourish you there? If you already approach the Bible that way, how has it changed you to do so?

4. What is one hope you have for how you might grow through reading this book?

How to Read the Bible:

An Overview

Not one letter, not one stroke of a letter, will pass from the Law until all is accomplished.

– Matthew 5:18

While this book is about biblical numbers, it is really about how to read the Bible. Our goal is to grow to understand biblical numbers, so that we become better readers of Scripture as a whole. Before diving into the numbers, we should take a step back and look at how to read the Bible by asking three important questions: "What is the Bible?", "What is the Bible for?," and, only then, "How do we read the Bible?" How we answer each of these questions will go a long way toward determining how we approach the Bible in general and the numbers in particular.

What is the Bible?

The Bible is the very word of God, the means by which God reveals himself. Drilling down a bit deeper, we can identify and defend specific properties of the Bible that shape how we read and understand it. Every theologian has a slightly different list of properties and may use slightly different terms, but they largely fall into four categories.

First, there is the *truth, certainty, and infallibility* of Scripture. Scripture reveals God truly and reliably. The seventeenth century Dutch theologian, Petrus van Mastricht, sums up our position nicely: "This general truth [about Scripture] implies certain specifics: its doctrinal and historical statements are most accurately consistent with the matter and the facts; its practical statements with the will of God; its prophecies, promises, and threats with the future event - no differently and no less than if they had been eyewitness testimonies. And that is the case because it has the God of truth as its author; Christ as the very truth it contains, and as its faithful witness; and the Holy Spirit, truth's infallible inspirer, as its guide."[3] In van Mastricht's time and ours, there are differences about how to handle more thorny issues in the Bible, but the initial assumption should always be that the Bible is a true and reliable witness.

Second, there is the *purity, holiness, perfection, and sufficiency* of Scripture. The Belgic Confession, Article 7 says that "We believe that this Holy Scripture contains the will of God completely and that everything one must believe to be saved is sufficiently taught in it."[4] We can know true things about God in Creation (known as the 'Book of Nature'), but it is only through the Book of Scripture that we come to

---

[3] Petrus van Mastricht, *Theoretical-Practical Theology, Volume 1: Prolegomena*, trans. Todd M. Rester, ed. Joel R. Beeke (Grand Rapids, MI: Reformation Heritage Books, 2018), 127.

[4] Belgic Confession, Article 7 from *Our Faith: Ecumenical Creeds, Reformed Confessions, and Other Resources* (Grand Rapids, MI: Faith Alive, 2013).

know salvation in Jesus Christ. When it comes to knowing who God is, what he has done, and who God has made us to be, God's Word is a sufficient source of that knowledge. Anywhere else we look will be insufficient for true knowledge of God. If the first property says the Bible is *reliable*, this one says the Bible is *enough*. It is holy and lacks nothing that we need for life and salvation. As John Calvin says, "it is better to limp along this path than to dash with all speed outside it."[5] The 'enough'-ness of the Bible does not mean we do not engage with tradition, or logic, or experience. But we never consider these as separate or independent sources of knowledge of God. Reason, tradition, and experience can, at times, be helpful guides, but it is never Scripture & Reason, Scripture & Tradition, or Scripture & Experience that forms our basis of knowledge of God and ourselves. This is what was meant by the Reformation slogan, *sola scriptura* ("Scripture alone"). Scripture alone is sufficient for knowing God and his salvation.

Third, there is the *perspicuity or efficacy* of Scripture. A less used, but perhaps better term is *clarity*. I like what Herman Bavinck says here, "Scripture speaks in the language of life, of the heart, of immediacy, of inspiration, and is thus understandable for every man, going forth into every generation, never growing old in its time, and therefore classic in the highest sense, in an utterly unique sense of the word."[6] Scripture is effective in accomplishing God's purposes for it. The Lord says, "As the rain and the snow come down from heaven, and do not return to it

---

[5] John Calvin, *The Institutes of Christian Religion*, trans. Ford Lewis Battles, ed. John T. McNeill (Philadelphia: Westminster Press, 1960), 1.VI.3.

[6] Herman Bavinck, *On Preaching & Preachers*, trans. & ed. James P. Eglinton (Peabody, Mass.: Hendrickson Publishers, 2017), 37-38.

without watering the earth and making it bud and flourish, so that it yields seed for the sower and bread for the eater, *so is my word that goes out from my mouth*: It will not return to me empty, but *will accomplish what I desire* and achieve the purpose for which I sent it." (Isaiah 55:10-11, italics for emphasis). Scripture is effective and clear; that is, it is able to be understood.

Understanding Scripture is not limited to the educated and the elite. This is one of the reasons that we will not be appealing directly to the original languages or to archaeological discoveries in this book. One way people can read the Bible profitably is to work to understand the meaning of the names and even make connections to the archaeological record. There is much to gain from that method (and I have personally been enriched by doing so), but we want to present a method that can be used by those without specialized knowledge. When our methods of reading Scripture, particularly the hard passages, depend too much upon specialized linguistic knowledge, we undermine the confidence of Christians to be able to read the Bible. This is not a critique of expertise at all. Instead, I am setting aside this valuable discipline in order to ask "What would help my mother's bible study to read these biblical numbers profitably?" How can we read the Bible well in such a way that demonstrates our trust in its clarity?

The Bible is not a labyrinth that can only be navigated by specialists, but the clear thread that leads us out of the confusing labyrinths of our (mis)understandings of God. This image of Scripture as the thread leading us out of the labyrinth comes from John Calvin: "For we should so reason that the splendor of the divine countenance, which even the apostle calls 'unapproachable' is for us like an inexplicable labyrinth unless we are conducted into it by the thread of the Word; so that it is better to limp along this path than to dash with all speed outside it."[7] Here, Calvin is drawing the picture from the story of Theseus in Greek Mythology. The hero Theseus was placed in a labyrinth with a Minotaur. The labyrinth was dark and complicated and created so that no one should be able to get out. However, the princess Ariadne gave Theseus a ball of red thread that he unrolled as he walked through the labyrinth. After killing the Minotaur, Theseus was able to follow the thread back and find his way out.

For Calvin, left to ourselves, our knowledge of God is like a labyrinth. It is full of twists and turns, truth and error, and something we can never escape on our own. By our own wit or wisdom, we cannot come to truly know God. God's "countenance" (or face) is "unapproachable." In our sin we will constantly twist any truth about God into something else. It is only if we are given a thread, the Word of God, that we will be led out of the labyrinth into true knowledge of God.

In addition to the labyrinth, Calvin also talks about a man limping and running, writing that it is better to limp along according to God's word than the run apart from it. It is not about the speed at which you move, but whether you are moving according to God's Word, according to the only means provided for you to come to God. Why is Scripture the only means? Because it holds forth Jesus Christ, our Redeemer, the Way, the Truth, and the Life. Even if you are limping in the Word, that is much better than running with all your might anywhere else.

While we value education and the use of original languages and grammar in studying the Bible, we also believe that the truth of Scripture is fundamentally clear

---

[7] Calvin, Institutes, 1.VI.3

and not hidden. The Bible's message is simple and clear enough for a child to understand, but deep enough that scholars can spend a lifetime studying it. This property guards against the Bible being metaphorically taken out of the hands of the people and kept only in the hands of pastors and professors.

Fourth, there is the *authority* of Scripture. We see this in Belgic Confession, Article 5, where the books of the Bible are received "for the regulating, founding, and establishing of our faith."[8] The content of our faith and shape of our lives as disciples are ruled by the Word of God. It is the norm, the standard, for our faith and life as Christians. We are governed, not by the whims of culture or by our feelings or by our desires, but by God's Word. For Christians, Scripture is also the *final* authority, the final court of appeals, so to speak, in any controversy on what we believe or how we live. In practical terms, if I read God's Word and, through study, am confident that I understand it correctly, but still don't like what it says, the problem is with me and not with the Word of God. That's one way that this authority of Scripture can function.

The first question that shapes how we interpret the Bible is "What is it?" We typically identify certain properties of Scripture that make a difference in how we read the Bible. I have grouped them in four categories: the *reliability* of Scripture, the *sufficiency* of Scripture, the *clarity* of Scripture, and the *authority* of Scripture. The second question we must answer before we can get to the practical dimension of how to read the Bible is this: What is it for?

What is the Bible for?

Purpose determines use. We use a wrench to turn bolts,

---

[8] Belgic Confession, Article 5.

not to hammer nails, because we know its purpose — to tighten or loosen a bolt. When someone hands me some chocolate and tells me that it is for my children, I now know what to do with the chocolate. I don't eat it myself, even if that seems like fun. I relate to it based upon the purpose for which it was given. In a similar way, knowing why Scripture was given will shape how we read it, how we relate to it, and what we do with it.

What is the Bible for? According to the Belgic Confession, the Scriptures were given "with special care for us and for our salvation."[9] Scripture was given 'for us.' By 'us,' we mean the church. Scripture was given to build up the church and to glorify God. When John Calvin argued for the Bible to be translated into the language of the common people, he used the image of the church as the school of Christ. The Bible should be in the hands of the people, in a language they can understand, so that we would grow in our ability to encourage and correct one another in the faith and thus grow as a church.[10] The natural home of the Bible is the church. God's Word is also an apologetic and evangelistic word, but its primary place is in the life of the church.

Scripture was also given "for our salvation." John 20:31 says "But these are written that you may believe that Jesus is the Messiah, the Son of God, and that by believing you may have life in his name." Scripture was given both to be received *by* faith in Christ and *for* faith in Christ. This includes knowledge of God and communion with God. It

---

[9] Belgic Confession, Article 3.
[10] Randall Zachman, "Learning to Read Scripture for Ourselves: The Guidance of Erasmus, Luther, and Calvin" in *The People's Book: The Reformation and the Bible*, eds. Jennifer Powell McNutt & David Lauber (Downer's Grove, IL: Intervarsity Press, 2017), 64-68.

involves repentance, faith, and trust in Jesus Christ. There is much to be learned through the Bible, but its primary purpose is that we might cling to Christ in faith. This purpose defines what we expect to find in the Bible.

How to read it?

With the properties and purpose of the Bible in place, how do we actually read it well? There is a basic pattern of reading that we might call "Whole-Part-Whole."

Step 1: Focus on the Whole

First, begin with prayer. Christian devotion and prayer are not casual add-ons to the process of reading the Bible, but absolutely central. Prayers for the work of the Holy Spirit and a vibrant life of Christian devotion and prayer are crucial for reading the Bible. The idea of being a "dispassionate observer" or trying to get objective distance is not a properly Christian way of reading the Bible. In short, trying to set aside prayer and Christian faith before reading the Bible is not reading the Bible *as* God's Word. Instead, reading the Bible as God's Word begins with prayer and faith in Christ.

Second, consult the tradition of interpreters as a guide, not an authority. We are never the first to read any passage of Scripture. We don't need to pretend to be. The sufficiency and clarity of Scripture does not mean that we never read any other books or that we cannot learn much from the reading of others. However, this great tradition of interpretation functions as a guide, not an authority. They are like wise elders we would do well to listen to, but with whom we do not always agree. John Calvin's commentaries are a good example of this. He regularly interacts with Augustine and Chrysostom's interpretation of a given passage. Sometimes he agrees with them, sometimes he disagrees, but he always listens and gives their interpretation respect.

Third, we assume the overall unity and coherence of Scripture. There are sixty-six different books in the Bible. Each author, under the inspiration of the Holy Spirit, writes differently, in a different context, and to a different original audience. Yet, because the ultimate author of Scripture is God and God does not contradict himself, the Bible is fundamentally coherent. The unity and coherence of Scripture is crucial for how we will read the Bible. For instance, the genealogies of Genesis not only tell us something about what is going on in the book of Genesis, but they can be set alongside genealogies in Matthew and Luke because the same Spirit inspired, shaped, and preserved both passages. Are there sometimes tensions between portions of the Bible? Yes. Are there contradictions? No. There are differences in different eras of salvation history - particularly between the Old and New Testaments - but there is a fundamental unity to God's Word. This unity shapes the process of using clear passages in Scripture to interpret more difficult ones, even if they are in a totally different part of the Bible. You can only do this if you believe in a fundamental unity of God's Word, that it speaks with one voice - God's.

Step 2: Pay attention to the Part

Next, we move from the whole to the part, the particular passage of Scripture you are studying. In looking at a particular passage of Scripture, there is great value in paying attention to the words in the original languages and the grammar of Greek, Hebrew, and Aramaic. Christians have frequently written word books, grammars, and dictionaries to help with the reading of Scripture. This volume will not focus on that particular work, but only the fruit of that work in English translations readily accessible to everyday Christians. Jesus tells us that not a stroke of a letter will pass away from the Law until all is accomplished (Mt 5:18). Every word and phrase in the Bible is there for a reason. Especially in a time where producing and preserving texts was extremely expensive, the fact that God preserved these details should force us to pay attention and contemplate them.

Thus, in a particular passage, we look at language and context, focusing on the plain sense of the text. Often, "plain sense" is equivalent to what is commonly called the "literal meaning" or "the intent of the author," but not always. Because the Bible is a coherent whole whose fundamental author is God, there are times when the literal meaning of a passage is not strictly a historical meaning, but a theological or Christological one. Sometimes the plain sense is the spiritual sense. We can occasionally draw together the literal and spiritual meanings of the text.[11] In short, when it comes to approaching an individual passage, we focus on reading a text in its literary, canonical, and theological context.

Step 3: Connect back to the Whole

Lastly, we move back to consider the whole by interpreting Scripture in light of other Scripture. This is the "canonical context," since we read Scripture in light of the whole canon - the entire Bible. It is here that we will most clearly see how the numbers connect the past, present, and future. Having looked closely at the details of the numbers and worked to get clear on their meaning, we will look at other places in the Bible where the same (or similar) events

---

[11] Craig G. Bartholomew, *Introducing Biblical Hermeneutics: A Comprehensive Framework for Hearing God in Scripture* (Grand Rapids, MI: Baker Academic, 2015), 198.

have happened or words have been used. Repetition in the Bible is God's way of drawing attention to something and creating connections. For example, Genesis 49 tells of the blessings on the sons of Israel. In Judah it says, "binding his foal to the vine, his donkey's colt to the choice vine." We should spend time trying to get the literal meaning of the text, but then asks, "where else have I seen this?" This takes us to Zechariah 9:9, "behold your king comes to you riding on a colt, the foal of a donkey" then to the triumphal entry of Jesus, where he comes in riding on a colt and foal. This question ('Where else have I seen this?') opens up the vistas of Scripture to help us see connections we would not have before. We interpret unclear passages in light of clear ones. Sometimes this means placing similar passages alongside each other, so that one clarifies the other. Other times it means placing texts that seem to be saying different things alongside each other to see what is causing the difference. Jesus tells us not to swear oaths, but Scripture frequently has godly people giving oaths or even being commanded to swear oaths by God's name. Tension, yes. Contradiction, no. So we have to interpret the unclear in light of the clear, determine what is similar and what is dissimilar. This method requires an intimate knowledge of the whole body of Scripture.

When reading the Bible, there are three questions we must answer. First, what is the Bible? It is the true, sufficient, clear, and authoritative word of God. Second, what is it for? Scripture was given for us, the church, and for our salvation. Lastly, how do we read it? We begin with the whole context of prayer, consulting the tradition, and the unity of Scripture. We then move to the details of the passage, considering language and context to determine the plain meaning of the passage. Finally, we move to the context of Scripture as a whole, considering how this passage might be interpreted in light of the rest of the Bible.

READING BIBLICAL NUMBERS

As we have already stated, each chapter will be unique, but the overall method will be the same. First, we will *pay attention to the details*, drilling down to the specifics of a passage and asking why God might have wanted us to know this information. Second, we will ask *where else have I seen this?* and draw connections between the number and the rest of Scripture. In reading this way, our hope is that you will grow not only in your appreciation for the numbers of the Bible, but as a reader of Holy Scripture as well.

Discussion Questions:

1. Do you agree with the list of properties of the Bible given in this chapter? What might you add? What might you change? Which property do you believe is most important?

2. How does the reason the Bible was written change how we read it? When have you experienced how the Bible is "for you and for your salvation"?

3. Describe your normal practice of reading the Bible. Where does this chapter resonate with what you are already doing? Where does this chapter challenge your normal practice?

Haven't I Seen That Somewhere Before?:

Repetition in the Bible

"What has been will be again, what has been done will be done again; there is nothing new under the sun."

– Ecclesiastes 1:9

"What an interesting thought — that much of the world finds the Bible less difficult to read than we do"

– Lois Tverberg

When Jesus was twelve years old, he went up to Jerusalem with his family for the Passover. It was likely a large family group that travelled like this every year, but something different happened on this trip. As they packed up and headed back to Galilee, the family assumed that Jesus was with them. They travelled for a whole day before they realized that he was missing. Distraught parents raced back to Jerusalem and spent three days looking for

Jesus. They found Jesus sitting in the temple, talking with the teachers.

Exasperated, Mary and Joseph told Jesus how worried they had been. Jesus' response already tells us that he knew something of his identity as the Son of God, "Why were you searching for me? Did you not know that I must be in my Father's house?" (Luke 2:49). In this passage we learn about more than just what Jesus thought about himself. We also learn what it means to be a student of the Bible.

As Jesus stayed behind in the temple, he sat among the teachers. These were experts in the Bible, people who devoted their life to understanding and teaching God's Word. Jesus' time in the temple was spent "listening to them and asking them questions. And all who heard him were amazed at his understanding and his answers" (Luke 2:46-47). Jesus asked really good questions. The depth of his understanding was seen in the kinds of questions he asked.

One of the ways we grow as students of the Bible is by learning to ask good questions. Good questions help us pay attention to the right details and listen for the right information. Good questions fit the passage we are studying and don't lead us off in unhelpful directions. In this chapter, we will look individually at the four key questions we should ask whenever we are studying the Bible and encounter a number of any kind:

1. Where else does this number appear in the Bible?
2. Does this passage continue or reverse the themes found in other passages that have this same number?
3. If this number does not repeat, are there other numbers associated with similar events?
4. Why was *this* number included in *this* passage?

Jesus demonstrated his understanding by asking good questions. With these questions in hand, our understanding of the Bible will grow and, Lord willing, we will grow as disciples of Jesus Christ.

Question 1: Where else does this number appear in the Bible?

The best place to look to understand the significance of a specific number in a bible passage is that bible passage itself. When Paul was performing miracles in Ephesus, there was a group of Jews who were going around trying to drive out evils spirits in the name of Jesus (even though they did not know Jesus). In Acts 19:14, it says that "Seven sons of Sceva, a Jewish chief priest, were doing this." Why does Acts record that there were seven sons of Sceva? The simplest answer is that this is what happened. A man named Sceva had seven sons and all seven of them were trying to cast out demons in the name of Jesus. Even as we try to delve deeper into the significance of the numbers, we should not miss the fact that these numbers are recorded because they are true.

However, God is sovereign over all and the Holy Spirit was active in inspiring the writers of Scripture. There are no accidents in biblical history or in the biblical account. So we can begin to ask some important questions: Why did God make it so that this man had seven sons? Why did God believe we needed to know he had seven sons (instead of just saying, "the sons of Sceva")?

Once we start to ask these questions, we often move beyond the specifics of one passage of the Bible. We are on safer ground, looking for an internal reference for a specific number, rather than an external one. In short, we are better off asking the significance of the number seven in the Bible than exploring the role of the number seven in the broader culture of the Ancient Near East. As always, there can be value in considering the results of archaeology and cultural study, but we are proposing a method that allows the everyday Christian to read more confidently without requiring specialized knowledge. Therefore, we should consider the significance of a particular number within the broader scope of the Bible. This leads us to our first key question: Where else does this number appear in the Bible?

Repetition in the Bible is an invitation to pay attention. Papyrus was expensive to produce and maintain. Many towns and synagogues could only afford one copy of the Scriptures for the whole community. Because of the incredible expense, there was no wasted space in the Scriptures. So if something was important enough to repeat, there was a reason. When we begin to look, we will see that the number seven is repeated throughout the Bible and in some very significant places. Here are a few:

- There are seven days of creation (Genesis 1:1-2:3).
- God himself is said to rest on the seventh day (Genesis 2:2-3).
- Every seven days, the people of God were to remember the Sabbath and rest from all their work (Exodus 20:8-11, Deuteronomy 5:12-15).
- The lampstand in the temple had seven lamps on it (Exodus 25:31-40).
- Naaman is told to wash in the Jordan river seven times (2 Kings 5:10).
- Jesus casts seven demons out of Mary Magdalene (Luke 8:2).
- Jesus feeds the four thousand with seven loaves (Mark 8:1-10).
- In the book of Revelation, there are seven spirits before the throne of God (Rev. 1:4).
- John is told to write letters to the seven churches after

seeing seven golden lampstands, which are the seven churches and seven stars which are said to be the angels of the seven churches (Rev. 1:12-20).
- The lamb in Revelation has seven horns and seven eyes (Rev. 5:6)
- In Revelation, there are seven seals (Rev. 5-8).
- Seven angels with seven trumpets (Rev. 8-11).
- John hears seven thunders (Rev. 10:3-4)
- The dragon has seven heads and seven crowns (Rev. 12:3).
- The beast has seven heads as well (Rev. 13:1).
- There are seven bowls of God's wrath (Rev. 16:1).[12]

Therefore, there must be some significance to us being told that Sceva had seven sons. In the next chapter, we will explore where to look for the central meaning of a biblical number. For our purposes here, though, simply note that when a number is repeated, it is a clue for us. Once we understand what the number seven tends to convey in the Bible, we will be better equipped to see what it means in the particular passage we are studying.

Seven is not the only number that is repeated regularly throughout the Bible. Nahor has twelve sons (Gen. 22:20-24), Ishmael has twelve sons (Gen. 25:12-18), then Jacob has twelves sons who become the twelve tribes of Israel (Gen. 35:23-26). Jesus chooses twelve disciples (Luke 6:12-16).

During the flood it rains for forty days and forty nights (Gen. 7:12), Moses spends forty years in Egypt, forty years tending sheep, and then leads Israel through the wilderness for forty years (Acts 7:23, 30, 36). Elijah spends forty days in the wilderness (1 Kings 19:8). Jesus spends forty days in the

---

[12] A whole study could be made just on the number seven in the book of Revelation (seven heads of the second beast are seven hills as well as seven kings — Rev. 17:9-10).

wilderness after his baptism by John in the Jordan (Mt. 4:2).

Abraham has two sons (Gen. 25:9; 1 Chr. 1:28), Isaac has two sons (Gen. 20:24-26), and Jesus tells a parable of a man who had two sons (Luke 15:11-32).

Three thousand are killed after the golden calf incident in the wilderness (Ex. 32:28). Three thousand are saved on Pentecost (Acts 2:41).

Jonah spends three days and three nights in the belly of a great fish (Jonah 1:17). Jesus spends three nights in the grave (Matt. 12:40; 1 Cor. 15:4; Luke 24:7).

These examples barely scratch the surface of all the repetition in the Bible. Not only are these numbers accurate, but they are providentially ordered by God to communicate something as well.

While there are tools that will help us find these repetitions — Bible software or concordances will give you all the instances of a given word in the Bible — this way of reading the Bible is best developed as a skill through regular reading and, if possible, memorizing parts of the Bible. The more you become familiar with the details of the Bible, the more these connections will come to you naturally.

QUESTION 2: DOES THIS PASSAGE CONTINUE OR REVERSE THE THEMES FOUND IN THE OTHER PASSAGES THAT HAVE THIS SAME NUMBER?

Simply knowing that a number is repeated throughout the Bible is not enough to understand its significance. Yes, there are a lot of "sevens" and "twelves" and "forties" in the Bible, but what exactly does that mean? First, we must determine the central meaning of a number within the context of the whole Bible. It is the burden of the next chapter to describe how to we do just that.

Then, we need to look at the particular passage we are studying and ask whether the usage of that number here continues the theme or pattern we see elsewhere or reverses that pattern. For instance, Jesus' forty days in the wilderness continues the pattern of wilderness periods for Moses, Israel, and Elijah throughout the Old Testament. It builds upon an existing theme. However, Jesus' command to Peter to forgive "seventy times seven" times (Mt. 18:22) reverses what we see from Lamech in Genesis 4, where he claims that those who injure him will receive "seventy times seven" vengeance (Gen. 4:24). Just because a number repeats does not mean it does the same thing. In particular, because the Bible is the story of God's redemption of people out of sin and bondage, some stories are specifically redemptive reversals of previous stories, which are highlighted by the repeated numbers. We will explore these reversals more fully in chapter four.

Question 3: If this number does not repeat, are there other numbers associated with similar events?

Sometimes we come across a number in the Bible that doesn't seem to repeat. Perhaps it is the census data in the book of Numbers (e.g. Numbers 26). Each tribe is listed with the number of people in it, but these numbers don't tend to repeat elsewhere in the Bible. Perhaps it is the dimensions of the temple or tabernacle — a long list of lengths and widths and numbers of pillars and hooks and twisted linen. In sections of the Bible where numbers don't seem to repeat, we need to change our strategies from looking for repetition to looking for comparison.

We should look at similar passages in the Bible and see if the numbers are larger, smaller, or the same. God tells the

Israelites how to build the tabernacle in the wilderness (Ex. 25–31). Solomon builds a temple (1 Kings 6). After that temple is destroyed and the people return from exile, they build a second temple (Ezra 3–6). Ezekiel is given a vision of the heavenly temple (Ezek. 40). In each of these instances, the exact dimensions described are different. The number of sacrifices used to dedicate the structure are different. Instead of asking the significance of the numbers themselves, we can ask why one temple was larger or smaller than another. We can ask the significance of the relative size and what God might have intended it to communicate.

Something similar can be done with the size of the tribes of Israel. There are twelve tribes, but each has a different number of descendants in the census. This is more than a fact of history. Instead, we can begin to ask why it would be important for us to know these exact numbers and why some tribes were bigger or smaller. How does their size connect with what they would be in the future or what God had promised about them in the past (Gen. 49:1-28)?

Our first instinct, when we come across a number in the Bible, should be to look for repetition in other passages in the Bible. However, when this doesn't yield much fruit, we should then turn our attention to similar situations in the Bible and look to compare the numbers. Why bigger? Why smaller? What might the difference mean? We will look at some examples of comparison in chapter six and develop some skills for making sense of them throughout the Bible.

QUESTION 4: WHY WAS THIS NUMBER INCLUDED IN THIS PASSAGE?

This last question is the most important. The goal of our study of biblical numbers is to read the Bible more faithfully and with greater confidence. However, faithful reading is about more than comprehension. Studying the numbers in the Bible is not about being clever or uncovering secret information. Rather, it is about paying attention in a new way so that we can grow to love God, love his Word, and love his people more faithfully. Faithful reading involves following the God who reveals himself in his Word. As Paul says, "knowledge puffs up while love builds up" (1 Cor. 8:1). We can gain all kinds of knowledge *about* God's Word, but if we do not then turn around and follow what it says, this knowledge has not truly transformed us. We might have *listened* to what the Bible says, but we did not truly *hear* it.

As we study these numbers in the Bible, we will be listening with an ear as to *why* God included these numbers here. As we have stated, there are no wasted words in the Bible. Every detail is included for a reason. Frequently, when the Spirit could have inspired the authors to write "many" or "few," the authors instead include specific numbers. In each of the subsequent chapters, we will wrestle with the meaning of these numbers, but also with their purpose within these passages.

At the heart of these handbooks is 1 Timothy 3:16, "All Scripture is God-breathed and is useful for teaching, reproof, correction, and training in righteousness." The goal of our study will not only for us to see clearly how God directed and inspired these numbers in history (and to be included in the Bible), but how they are *useful* for our faith in Christ. A deeper understanding of the numbers in the Bible should lead us deeper in our journey of discipleship to Jesus Christ.

Therefore, in addition to asking all the questions that illuminate the biblical numbers directly, we must always end our study with pausing and thinking through the practical implications of these insights for our walk with Jesus.

CONCLUSION

Even at twelve years old, Jesus demonstrated his understanding by asking good questions. As disciples of Jesus, we grow in our understanding of the Bible when we learn to ask good questions. In this chapter, we looked at how repetition is a clue to pay attention by asking, "Where else does this number appear in the Bible?" But we also saw how it is not enough to know that a number repeats, as we need to see whether this passage continues or reverses themes seen elsewhere in the Bible. We also looked at what questions to ask when looking for repetition seems to fail. We saw that comparing different numbers in similar situations can lead to surprising insights. We ended our questions by recognizing that studying the Bible is not just about growing in knowledge, but about growing in faithfulness. We must keep our walk with God front and center whenever we read, so that the understanding we gain will impact our life of faith.

So far, we have painted the picture of how to understand biblical numbers with broad brush strokes. However, in the chapters that follow, we will work out the finer details of each of these questions through very specific examples.

Discussion Questions:

1. Which do you prefer: good questions or good answers? Why? What value might each have for reading the Bible?

2. What strategies do you use when you encounter a confusing passage in the Bible?

3. In the last chapter, we suggested that reading the Bible should begin with a posture of prayer. What would you like to pray for when you start reading the Bible?

Finding the Center:

Understanding Repeated Numbers

"And beginning with Moses and all the Prophets, he explained to them what was said in all the Scriptures concerning himself."

– Luke 24:27

"The more we see the connections between the Testaments, the less likely we are to succumb to the idea that the God of the Old Testament is morally inferior to or must be distinguished from the God revealed in Jesus."

– Alistair Roberts & Andrew Wilson

We are tempted to read the Bible as a set of disconnected texts. The way our Bibles are set up unintentionally encourages this practice. There are several (mostly) blank pages sitting between the Old and New Testaments. Each of the sixty-six books is separated from the others. Headings, chapters, and verses have been added throughout the centuries. While these additions have, in many ways, made it easier to read and find things in the Bible, they have also, in many ways, made it harder to read it as intended. The Bible is one book, a cohesive whole. Though the Bible was written over many centuries by many different human authors, the same Holy Spirit was at work in and through each of those authors. Seeing each verse isolated from the others cuts us off from one of the greatest resources for understanding the Bible — the Bible itself.

Seeing connections between passages of the Bible is a crucial skill for growing in understanding the Bible. While we are focusing on repeated biblical numbers in this book, these connections are in no way limited to numbers. However, just because there is a connection between two passages does not mean we know what it means. In this chapter, we will answer the crucial question: How do we understand what a repeated number actually means?

Explanation of Principle: Where do we look to understand what this repeated number means?

Repetition is a clue to pay attention in the Bible. The more you read and contemplate the Scriptures, the more often details from one passage will begin to feel familiar and remind you of another passage. These connections are a vital resource for diving deeper into understanding the Bible. This is particularly true when it comes to the numbers in the Bible. Once you begin to look, numbers like seven, twelve, and forty seem to appear everywhere. Looking for repetition is the most common and most important practice for understanding biblical numbers.

However, noticing that numbers repeat is not enough. It might be fascinating to realize that two passages from very different parts of the Bible record something with the exact same number, but what does it mean? Why is it important?

We need to figure which passage provides the best context for understanding the meaning of this number in the others. Out of all the references to seven, twelve, or forty, which passage provides the center of meaning? Each passage should be read in all its unique particularity and with reference to its context within its particular book. However, the canonical context is also important, particularly when we want to understand the echoes and resonances between various passages and themes (including numbers). Once we have determined which passage sits at the center of meaning for a given number, we can then evaluate how other instances fit within the broader meaning of that number in Scripture.

There are three main places we should look for the central meaning of a repeated biblical number: the first instance, the Exodus, or Jesus. For some numbers, the first time it appears in the Bible is huge clue about how we are to understand it every other time it appears. For others, God's work of salvation in bringing his people out of Egypt is the central passage which echoes both backward and forward throughout the Bible. While all of Scripture finds its fulfillment in Jesus, some numbers find their central meaning in the birth, life, death, and resurrection of Jesus Christ. Many of the repeated numbers will continue the same theme or meaning almost every they appear in the Bible. A select few, however, will have opposite meanings in different places (which we will talk about in the next chapter).

Determining the central story for the meaning of a biblical number is more a matter of wisdom than technique. Some numbers will be obvious, while others will require significant time wrestling, studying, and praying before God reveals an insight. Let's look at each of these three places where numbers can find their central meaning and then work through some examples to help us see how this might work for numbers that have not been included in this book.

First Instance: The Seven Days of Creation & Seventy Nations

One place we look for the central meaning of a number is the first time it appears in the Bible. We then can read the other instances in light of its meaning in this first passage. As we have already seen in the previous chapter, seven is one of the most common and repeated numbers throughout the Bible — appearing from Genesis to Revelation. Understanding the significance of the number seven within the Bible will open up new insights and depths of interpretation for a variety of passages.

"Seven" is an example of where the *first time* it shows up in the Bible is key for grasping its overall significance. The very first story in the whole Bible contains the number "seven." In Genesis 1, God spends six days making the heavens and the earth. He creates light and darkness, sea and sky, fish and birds, plants and animals. At the pinnacle of the sixth day, God creates human beings. "So God created humankind in his image, in the image of God he created them; male and female he created them" (Gen. 1:27). However, the capstone of the entire creation account is not the creation of humans, but the seventh day. God created in six days, but the creation account is seven full days.

> "Thus the heavens and the earth were finished,
> and all their multitude. And on the seventh day
> God finished the work that he had done, and he

rested on the seventh day from all the work that he had done. So God blessed the seventh day and hallowed it, because on it God rested from all the work that he had done in creation" (Gen. 2:1-3)

Creation was completed by God resting. It was not finished until God chose to cease his work and declare the work complete. Rest as the pinnacle of creation has a lot to say to us about the role of sabbath in the life of faith, but this story gives "seven" a particular significance. It symbolizes creation that is "finished" or "complete." Because God completed creation in seven days, seven is a complete number of something in the Bible. Whenever "seven" is mentioned, it not only refers to a literal number of things, but communicates that the amount is complete, perfect, or full.

With this idea that seven means "completeness," many of the other sevens in the Bible start to come into focus more clearly. Every seven days, the people were to celebrate the sabbath by resting from their labors (like God did on the seventh day — Ex. 20:8-11; Dt. 5:12-15). The sabbath is not a break from activity so that you can recharge for work, but it is the fullness or completion of the week. Rest completes work. Every seven years, the land and people are called to rest and people are released from the debt (Lev. 25; Dt. 15:2). This represents the fullness of years and people are to be given complete freedom. It also ties closely to the sabbath principle of rest (and freedom) as the pinnacle of the work of creation. Whether the seventh day of the week, or the seventh year, seven represents a fullness or completeness of time.

Pharaoh dreams of seven fat, sleek cows being eaten up by seven poor, ugly, and thin cows, then of seven good ears of grain being swallowed up by seven thin ears (Gen. 41:14-24). Joseph interprets these as referring to seven years of plenty followed by seven years of famine. In both cases, seven is both literal and symbolic. Egypt has seven years of plenty, but they also experience complete abundance. "So Joseph stored up grain in such abundance — like the sand of the sea — that he stopped measuring it; it was beyond measure" (Gen. 41:49). Yet, Egypt also experienced seven years of famine — a complete and utter famine. "Moreover, all the world came to Joseph in Egypt to buy grain, because the famine became severe throughout the world" (Gen. 41:57). Both plenty and famine were experienced in their fullness.

Naaman is told to wash in the Jordan river seven times (2 Kings 5:10). In this way, he was told not just to wash once, but to wash completely. Jesus casts seven demons out of Mary Magdalene (Luke 8:2). He removes a full set of demons from her and completely sets her free. The book of Revelation is full of the number seven and the whole book shows the fullness of God's plan for the end of all things, when creation and all God's purposes will finally be complete. Therefore, the seven churches represent the fullness of the church (Rev. 1:12-3:22). This is why their various experiences, challenges, encouragements, and rebukes are as much for the church today as in the first century. The lamb has seven eyes, because it sees completely (Rev. 5:6). There are seven trumpets, seven bowls, and seven seals because these represent the completion or fulfillment of God's will and judgment upon the earth. Each of the sevens in the book of Revelation is symbolic of something experienced completely or in its fullness.

Another example of a number's first appearance

carrying its meaning is the number seventy. Seventy is a combination of two numbers (7x10 — more on number combinations in a chapter five), and also carries the sense of a total number of something. While seven symbolizes completeness in the sense of perfection, seventy means complete in the sense of a full amount or full number. We see seventy appear first in Genesis 10 in the genealogy of Noah's sons. Sometimes called the "Table of Nations," this genealogy lists seventy nations or cities that come from Noah's children. These covered what was considered the known world at the time. In this way, the seventy nations symbolize the full number of nations in the world. The other instances of seventy follow similar patterns. There are seventy sons of Jacob who come down to Egypt (Gen. 46:27) — a full amount of the children of Jacob. The parallel possibly runs deeper as well. The seventy sons of Noah cover every nation on the earth. God promised Abraham that "I will indeed bless you and I will make your offspring as numerous as the stars of heaven and as the sand that is on the seashore" (Gen. 22:17). Jacob, who bears the covenant of Abraham, having the same number of family come into Egypt as the nations of the earth, is the beginning of the fulfillment of God's promise to Abraham.

The seventy years in exile for Judah would carry the same symbolism — it is a full amount of years to be cut off and separated from the land of promise (Jer. 25:11). The seventy disciples that Jesus sends out two-by-two would also parallel the seventy nations, the seventy children of Jacob, and the fullness of number[13] of disciples (Luke 10:1-

---

[13] This fullness of number is always symbolic and not strictly literal. While Jesus literally sent out seventy disciples, its symbolic meaning of "full number" does not mean that Jesus must literally have seventy disciples. The same is true of the 144,000 in the book of Revelation (Rev. 7:1-8; 14:3). The number

12).

The first instance of a number in the Bible can sometimes determine its symbolic meaning throughout the Scriptures. In my reading, this is the least common place to find the central meaning, but it does incorporate one of the most important and repeated numbers in the Bible — seven.

THE EXODUS: FORTY YEARS AND TEN PLAGUES

The next two places to look for the central meaning of a biblical number are the two central salvation stories of the Bible — the Exodus and Christ. The Exodus, the great saving work of God in the Old Testament, points to and prefigures the greater saving event of God in Jesus Christ. Because of how deeply connected these two events are in the Bible, sometimes there is slippage between the two when trying to discern the center of meaning. However, we will look at two examples of key numbers that find their meaning primarily in the Exodus — forty and ten.

After God delivered his people from Egypt, they spent forty years in the wilderness. This forty-year period was both a time of trial and wandering from God (Ps. 95:7-11) as well as a time of deep intimacy with God (Jer. 2:1-3).[14] Israel grumbled against God, but it was also like their honeymoon after the marriage on Mount Sinai. These twin experiences are held together throughout the forty years — closeness to God and struggle, trial and renewal, intimacy and purification.

These two themes carry over when we think about the other instance of forty in the Bible. When God saw that "the

---

is symbolic of the fullness of Jew and Gentile (12 x 12 x 1000) and is not intended as a literal number of those who are saved.

[14] For more on the wilderness as both wandering and intimacy, see Stephen C. Shaffer, *Rooted: Growing in Christ in a Rootless Age* (Peniel Press: 2022), p. 118ff.

wickedness of humankind was great upon the earth, and that every inclination of the thoughts of their hearts was only evil continually" (Gen. 6:5), he sent a flood upon the earth. For God said, "I will blot out from the earth the human beings I have created" (Gen. 6:7). This flood came in the form of rain for forty days and forty nights. The flood was a judgment upon the wickedness of humanity, but it was also a purification and cleansing of creation. Like the forty years in the wilderness was a process of cleansing Israel from its time in Egypt, the forty days of rain cleansed and purified the creation. Yet, both periods of forty were also places for renewal. On the other side of the flood was God's covenant with Noah and Noah worshipping the Lord (Gen. 8:20-9:17). There were problems on the far side of the flood (Gen. 9:20-29), but it was a time of renewal and purification.

Moses' life can be divided into three periods of forty years. He spends forty years in Egypt (Acts 7:23), and then forty years in the Midian tending his father-in-law's flocks (Acts 7:30), before living his final forty years with Israel in the wilderness (Acts 7:36). He spends forty days and nights on Mount Sinai (Ex. 32). These periods share the same themes as before — purification and renewal, intimacy with God and trial.

These themes become even more pronounced for Elijah and Jesus, both of whom spend forty days in the wilderness. Like Israel before him, Elijah grumbled and wanted to give up on the mission that God had given him. He seemed alone and it all felt like too much. But then he was fed miraculously in the wilderness (like manna?) and was strengthened for forty days and forty nights and then came to the mountain of God (1 Kgs. 19:4-9). Here, God told Elijah to stand before him and Elijah beheld the presence of

God in sheer silence (1 Kgs. 19:11-18). For Elijah, his wilderness time of forty days and forty nights was one of trial as well as one of intimacy with God and a renewal of his calling and mission.

The same is true for Jesus. Following his baptism by John in the Jordan, Jesus is led by the Spirit into the wilderness (Mt. 4:1-11). This is a period of trial for Jesus, where he is tempted by the devil three times. In each instance, Jesus relies on the Word of God to resist the devil, who eventually flees from him. Among other things, these temptations from Satan are a trial for Jesus, determining whether he will follow through on his mission when it becomes difficult. However, unlike Israel, Moses, and Elijah, Jesus does not grumble in the wilderness. He experiences trials and difficulty, but they come from outside of him, not from within himself. Where the periods of forty *before* Jesus were times of trial and struggle (and, occasionally, failure), Jesus emerges victorious.

Another number that finds its central meaning in the Exodus is the number ten. God uses ten plagues to break the power of Pharaoh and rescue his people from Egypt (Ex. 7:14–12:32). The final plague (the tenth) takes place on the tenth day of the month, which becomes the celebration of the Passover (Ex. 12:3). After delivering the Israelites, God brings them up to Mount Sinai, where he gives them the Ten Commandments, a summary of his Law for his people (Ex. 20:1-17).

These stories connect the number ten with both God's Law and God's judgment and worship. Ten makes clear what God requires and ten rejects all false worship and extols the supreme worship of the Lord. Thus, it should be no surprise that this number comes up again and again in relationship to worship in the temple and the offerings to

God. There were ten curtains in the Tabernacle (Ex. 26). Ten showed up already in the flood story ("waters receded until the tenth day of the tenth month" — Gen. 8:5), which is a judgment upon the world for disobedience to the commands of God. Giving a tenth (or 'tithe') is part of worshipping God and giving him what we owe to him (Lev. 27:30; cf. Gen. 14:20; 28:22). Sodom and Gomorrah would have been saved from judgment if there were only ten righteous people (Gen. 18:32). While in the wilderness, God provides the people with manna, and the people are to take one omer of manna per person (Ex. 16). However, there is a curious detail mentioned — "(an omer is a tenth of an ephah)" (Ex. 16:36). God gives the people a tenth in the wilderness to eat each day. The people are called to give a tenth to God in worship as an offering. When the people are commanded to offer a lamb every day in sacrifice (read: worship) to the Lord, they are also commanded to offer a tenth of an ephah of flour mixed with oil (Ex. 29:40). The same amount of flour was offered every day as the amount of manna they received in the wilderness. In both cases, they offered a tenth in worship.

The ten plagues and the ten commandments connect the number ten with God's judgment and commandments, which center on the proper worship of God. For this reason, we see a lot of tens related to the temple, tithing, and the worship of the Lord.

JESUS: THE CENTER OF EVERYTHING

The most important event in the history of the world is the life, death, and resurrection of Jesus Christ. One of the best ways to understand a biblical number is to see what it means in stories in the life of Jesus. We will look at only two examples, since many of the others will show up in other places in this handbook.

Jesus died on the cross and rose again on the third day. Many instances of three in the Bible point to the death and resurrection of Jesus. The most prominent example was named by Jesus himself — Jonah.

> "Then some of the scribes and Pharisees said to him, 'Teacher, we wish to see a sign from you.' But he answered them, 'An evil and adulterous generation asks for a sign, but no sign will be given to it except the sign of the prophet Jonah. For just as Jonah was for three days and three nights in the belly of the sea monster, so for three days and three nights the Son of Man will be in the heart of the earth." (Mt. 12:38-40)

Jonah's three days in the belly of the fish symbolize the three days Jesus spent in the tomb. Just as Jonah was delivered out onto the shore, Jesus Christ rose up from death. Though there are select references to three that may hint at the three persons of the Trinity (Gen. 18:1-11, though this is debated), the majority should be read in light of the death and resurrection of Jesus Christ.

There is some overlap between the Exodus and Jesus on the number twelve. There are twelve sons of Jacob who form the twelve tribes of Israel (Gen. 35:23-26). Many of the twelves in the Old Testament are clear references to those twelve tribes. Jesus selects twelve disciples (Luke 6:12-16). This is intentional. These twelve disciples constitute a renewed and reformed people of God. Just as the twelve tribes (and the number twelve) previously symbolized the people of God, the twelve disciples (and twelve in the New Testament) symbolize those who follow as disciples of Jesus Christ. In both cases, twelve refers to the covenant people of

God; in the Old Testament it refers to the covenant people of Abraham (by birth), and in the New Testament it refers to the covenant people of Abraham (by faith in Jesus). These are related as promise and fulfillment and the symbolism overlaps.

Conclusion

One of the most common and most important tools for understanding the numbers in the Bible is to find where a specific number repeats elsewhere in the Bible. However, that is not enough. We must know what that number means in the Bible more generally in order to see its significance in the particular passage we are studying. We have looked at examples of three different places to look for the primary meaning of a biblical number: its first appearance in the Bible; in the exodus from Egypt; and in the life, death, and resurrection of Jesus Christ. Once we determine the central meaning, we will be better equipped to see its significance everywhere. However, not every number continues the same theme throughout the Bible. Sometimes, one story will reverse the meaning of another. We will explore this in the next chapter.

Discussion Questions:

1. Practice making connections. Read Matthew 18:21-35. What details do you now notice? What questions do you have? What other passages come to mind?

2. Recall a time where reading one bible passage made you think of another? What was the passage? What was that experience like?

3. Share a time where reading the Bible brought you joy. Describe the experience.

4. Share a time where reading the Bible "cut you to the heart" (Acts 2:38). Describe the experience.

Mourning Into Dancing:

Reversal and Redemption

"He provided redemption for his people; he ordained his covenant forever— holy and awesome is his name."

– Psalm 111:9, NIV

"You turned my wailing into dancing; you removed my sackcloth and clothed me with joy"

– Psalm 30:11, NIV

The past does not always determine the future. There is incredible value in paying attention to history. We find the same struggles, same patterns, same issues cropping up again and again across the pages of history. When we fail to learn from history, we are prone to the same failures as our ancestors.

The same is true within families. The same patterns, struggles, and issues can come up generation after generation, as trauma, abuse, or suffering cascade down from parent to child. We learn a lot about who we are as families, as individuals, and as a people by looking back at who we were or where we have been.

However, sometimes there is healing and redemption. Patterns can be reversed. Broken people can be healed. The path of an individual or family can be turned from darkness to light. In this chapter, we will see how God's work of redemption can be seen in how he reverses the central symbolic meaning of certain numbers in the Bible. In this chapter, we will work through three examples of how God took a number with one meaning and then redeemed it in a latter passage in the Bible.

THE REDEMPTION OF NUMBERS

The Bible is a story of redemption. After Adam and Eve sinned and were cast out of the Garden, creation entered into bondage to sin. Death became the fate of every person. Our hearts were turned away from God. All was not as it should be.

Yet, God did not leave us in sin, but came to rescue and redeem us. In Jesus Christ, God flipped the script on the human race. Instead of wicked, Jesus was righteous. Instead of disobedient, Christ obeyed completely. Instead of pouring out malice, Christ was full of compassion. Instead of taking advantage of and exploiting the poor, Christ raised them from the dust. Jesus set the captives free. He gave sight to the blind. He made the lame to walk. He entered the depths of death and took on the full weight of sin, but was raised to victorious life.

The Bible is a story of redemption. Just because something has always been this way does not mean it has to remain that way. God redeems in Jesus Christ.

Not every number in the Bible is a sign of faithfulness. There are patterns of sin and disobedience in the Bible that show up in repeated numbers. Yet, sometimes we will see God redeem even the numbers in the Bible. He will take the pattern of a particular number and turn it around, redeem it.

Repetition is a clue for us to pay attention in the Bible. However, noticing that a number repeats is only the first step. In many cases, the numbers follow a similar pattern throughout their appearance in the Bible. However, we should also keep our eyes and ears open for when God is reversing the course of a previous story. The repeated number is a clue that we should see these two stories as connected. Yet, instead of the second story continuing the pattern of the first, it does something quite different. When this happens, we should ask the second of our four key questions: **Does this passage continue or reverse the themes found in the other passages that have this number?** Let's look at three key examples of the pattern of reversal in Scripture.

How Many Times?: Vengeance and Forgiveness

After Adam and Eve trust the lies of the serpent and eat from the tree of the knowledge of good and evil, they are cast out of the garden. Sin has entered the world and is worming its way into every nook and cranny of creation. In the aftermath, Adam and Eve have two sons: Cain and Abel. One day, both of them present their offerings to the Lord. Cain brings the fruit of the ground, while Abel brings the fat portions of the best of his flock. The Lord is pleased with Abel's offering, but not as much with Cain's. Cain becomes angry. God warns him about sin crouching at his door, but Cain does not heed the warning. He lures his brother out into a field and kills him. When asked about his brother's location, Cain replies, "I do not know; am I my brother's keeper?" (Gen. 4:10). The relationship between the first two brothers ends in jealousy and murder.

Cain has a son, Enoch, who has his own son, Irad. Irad has Mehujael. Mehujael has Methushael, and Mathushael has Lamech. Five generations are recorded until we get to Lamech. Cain, whose line began with jealousy and murder, culminates in Lamech. In Genesis 4:23-24, we encounter a significant number connected with Lamech:

"Lamech said to his wives:
"Adah and Zillah, hear my voice;
 You wives of Lamech, listen to what I say:
I have killed a man for wounding me,
 A young man for striking me.
If Cain is avenged sevenfold,
 Truly Lamech seventy-sevenfold."

Lamech has been disproportionate in his response to injury. When he is simply wounded, he responds by killing the other person. When someone strikes him on the face, he ends that person's life. He claims that his ancestor, Cain, had sevenfold vengeance on those who harmed him. Sevenfold, meaning full and complete revenge. However, Lamech goes above and beyond. He will be avenged seventy-seven times. For one small injury, Lamech will pay out incredible violence and retribution. This is the legacy of Cain. Not just complete revenge, but over-the-top violence upon anyone for any injury at all.

Seventy-seven times. Where else do we find that number in the Bible?

In Matthew 18, Peter comes to Jesus asking a question about forgiveness in the church. "Lord, if another member of the church sins against me, how often should I forgive? As many as seven times?" (Mt. 18:21). Peter asks about the limits of forgiveness and gives what would have seemed a good and generous answer. We should forgive someone seven times for sinning against us. As we have seen, this would have meant a full and complete forgiveness. However, Jesus' response would have drawn Peter (and should draw us) back to the story of Lamech. "Jesus said to him, 'Not seven times, but, I tell you, seventy-seven times'" (18:22). [15]

While Lamech proclaimed a seventy-sevenfold vengeance on anyone who injured him, Jesus proclaimed a seventy-sevenfold forgiveness for anyone who sins against us in the church. Both begin with the reality of being injured by another (physically, spiritually, emotionally, or otherwise). However, they are very different responses. The pathway of Cain and Lamech is jealousy and violence, while the pathway of Jesus is mercy and forgiveness. In this way, Jesus takes the root meaning of seventy-seven (extravagant, overabundant, boundless) and reverses it. Disciples of Jesus are called to practice forgiveness with the same level of extravagance as Lamech practiced revenge. The way of Jesus reverses the way of Cain and the two stories are connected through the presence of the same number — seventy-seven.

THE LORD ADDED TO THEIR NUMBER: DEATH AND SALVATION

When God brings the people out of Egypt and across the Red Sea, he leads them through the wilderness to the foot of Mount Sinai. Moses goes up on Mount Sinai to meet with God, while the people waited at the foot of the mountain. God gives Moses detailed instructions about the construction of the tabernacle as well as the basics of how

---

[15] Some translations have "seventy times seven."

Israel was to live before God as his covenant people. Chapter after chapter is filled with instructions as God establishes his relationship with his people through a covenant.

However, all this takes a long time. The people grow impatient waiting for Moses. They go to Aaron and say, "Come, make gods for us, who shall go before us; as for this Moses, the man who brought us up out of the land of Egypt, we do not know that has become of him" (Ex. 32:1). Aaron tells them to take off their gold rings, forms a mold and makes the image of a calf, saying, "These are your gods, O Israel, who brought you up out of the land of Egypt!" (Ex. 32:4). Aaron also makes an altar and the next day a festival is declared. The people bring sacrifices and begin to revel.

God is not pleased. He threatens to destroy the people for their idolatry and build a new nation through Moses. Moses intercedes and the Lord sends him down the mountain, carrying the two tablets of the covenant with God. When Moses sees what the people have done, he breaks the tablets (a visual sign that the covenant has been broken), destroys the calf, and makes the people drink the powder mixed with water (Ex. 32:19-20). Aaron blames the people and claims that the calf miraculously walked out of the fire when they threw in their gold (Ex. 32:22-24). As the events unfold, there is a curious detail — a number — that will connect with another story in the Bible:

> "Then Moses stood in the gate of the camp, and said, "Who is on the LORD's side? Come to me!" And all the sons of Levi gathered around him. He said to them, "Thus says the LORD, the God of Israel, 'Put your sword on your side, each of you! Go back and forth from gate to gate throughout the camp, and each of you kill your

brother, your friend, and your neighbor.'" The sons of Levi did as Moses commanded, and *about three thousand of the people fell on that day.* Moses said, "Today you have ordained yourselves for the service of the LORD, each one at the cost of a son or a brother, and so have brought a blessing on yourselves this day." (Ex. 32:25-29, emphasis added)

This should have been a day of celebration. God had brought his Law, established his covenant with his people. Yet, on that very day, it was already broken by the people worshipping false gods. To add to this tragedy, three thousand died at the foot of Mount Sinai as God's judgment on the people.

Three thousand are killed. Where else in the Bible do we find the number three thousand?

The day God gave the Law on Mount Sinai was commemorated down through the ages in the feast of Pentecost. It was not only a feast of the first fruits of the harvest, but a reminder of the gift of God's Law. On one Pentecost, after Jesus had died and risen from the grave, something amazing happened.

"When the day of Pentecost had come, they were all together in one place. And suddenly from heaven there came a sound like the rush of a violent wind, and it filled the entire house where they were sitting. Divided tongues, as of fire, appeared among them, and a tongue rested on each of them. All of them were filled with the Holy Spirit and began to speak in other languages, as the Spirit gave them ability" (Acts 2:1-4)

As God gave his Law long ago on Pentecost, now he

pours out his Holy Spirit upon the church. People are confused, wondering if they are drunk ("reveling" like back in Exodus 32). Peter responds with a powerful sermon tracing how the events of that day were the fulfillment of God's Word and proclaiming Jesus as God's promised Messiah. Those hearing the sermon are cut to the heart and wonder how they should respond to this message.

> "Peter said to them, "Repent, and be baptized every one of you in the name of Jesus Christ so that your sins may be forgiven; and you will receive the gift of the Holy Spirit. For the promise is for you, for your children, and for all who are far away, everyone whom the Lord our God calls to him." And he testified with many other arguments and exhorted them, saying, "Save yourselves from this corrupt generation." So those who welcomed his message were baptized, and that day *about three thousand were added.* They devoted themselves to the apostles' teaching and fellowship, to the breaking of bread and the prayers." (Acts 2:38-42, emphasis added)

On the first Pentecost, the covenant of God was broken by the people and three thousand were killed. The first Pentecost was a day of tragedy and death. However, on the later Pentecost, God poured out his Spirit and three thousand were saved. The second Pentecost is a day of salvation and life. At the first Pentecost, the people ate and drank and began to revel. At the second Pentecost, they are not drunk on wine, but filled with the Holy Spirit.

The same number appears in both stories, which is a clue to read them side-by-side. When we set Pentecost and Sinai next to each other, we see how Pentecost reverses the earlier story. The festival itself experiences resurrection as the Spirit brings salvation where there had once been death. In both stories, three thousand people are changed. In the former, they are moved from life to death. In the latter, they are moved from dead in sin to alive in Christ by the Spirit. The number three thousand serves as the connecting point that shows God's redemptive work among his people.

Do You Love Me?: Denial and Restoration

The night of Jesus' arrest is one of the most tragic and disorienting nights in his disciples' lives. Despite Jesus telling them plainly that he will be betrayed and crucified (and rise again on the third day), they do not see it coming. The Twelve gather together for the Passover meal. Jesus says again that he will be betrayed and that his disciples will all desert him that very night. Jesus says to Peter:

> "Simon, Simon, listen! Satan has demanded to sift all of you like wheat, but I have prayed for you that your own faith may not fail; and you, when once you have turned back, strengthen your bothers." And he said to him, "Lord, I am ready to go with you to prison and to death!" Jesus said, "I tell you, Peter, the cock will not crow this day, until you have denied three times that you know me" (Luke 22:31-34)

Jesus prophesies that Peter will deny him three times, and three times Peter says that he does not know Jesus. The third time we hear, "But Peter said, "Man, I do not know what you are talking about!" At that moment, while he is still speaking, the cock crows. The Lord turns and looks at Peter. Then Peter remembers the word of the Lord, how he had said to him, ""Before the cock crows today, you will deny me three times." And he went out and wept bitterly"

(Lk. 22:60-62). It all happens just as Jesus had promised.

Three times is a very specific number. In this instance, it is probably not helpful to try and see how this instance of "three" connects with every other "three" in the Bible, but to ask more specifically, "where else does three appear in the life of Peter?"

The next day after Jesus' trial and Peter's denial, Jesus is crucified. Three days later, he rises from the dead. The women find the empty tomb and tell the disciples. Peter races to the tomb and finds it empty. Jesus appears to the disciples over the next days, proving himself to be alive.

However, not long after this, Peter gathers several of the other disciples and they go fishing. Peter had been a fisherman when Jesus told him to leave his nets and follow him (Mt. 4:18-20). Now, having denied Jesus three times, Peter is back to fishing. Some suggest that Peter goes fishing because he wants to be where he first met Jesus, in the hopes of meeting him there again. Yet, I tend to think that Peter has gone back to his old life. He has failed as a disciple. He proclaimed that he would follow Jesus anywhere, even to death, but when the pressure was on, Peter failed.

The whole night, they catch nothing. Just after daybreak, Jesus stands on the beach and calls for them to cast their nets on the right side of the boat. Once they do, the net is filled with fish. The disciples realize it is Jesus and head swiftly to shore. Peter doesn't wait for the boat to get there, for he jumps into the sea in his urgency to see Jesus.

Jesus already has his own breakfast of fish ready and he invites the disciples to join him. During their conversation, the number three repeats. We are told, "This was now the third time that Jesus appeared to the disciples after he was raised from the dead" (John 21:14). Most significantly, Jesus asks Peter the same question three times. "Simon son of

John, do you love me more than these?" (John 21:15, 16, 17). Why three times? How many times did Peter say that he didn't know Jesus? How many times does Jesus ask Peter whether he loved him?

I think it is no accident that both events take place three times. This is a story of restoration for Peter. He is still a disciple of Jesus. He may have thought his failure meant that his time as a disciple was done and he should return to his old life and go back to his nets. However, Jesus still has a place for a failed disciple like Peter. Jesus still wants to know if Peter loves him. Jesus still calls Peter. "Jesus said to him, 'Feed my lambs'" (John 21:15). The presence of the three questions of Jesus connects back to the three denials of Peter. The restoration of Peter is signaled by the same threefold pattern.

Conclusion

This pattern of reversal is good news for all of us. Just because our life has gone down one path does not mean God cannot redeem it and turn it around. Jesus took the pattern of vengeance seen in Lamech and turned it into a pattern of forgiveness — extravagant and over-the-top. The Spirit took the pattern of disobedience, idolatry, and judgment seen at the foot of Mount Sinai and turned it into the redemption through the Gospel on Pentecost. Jesus took Peter's denials, turned them around, and restored him as a beloved disciple of Jesus.

A repeated number is a clue to pay attention. Yet, sometimes what we see is not the continuing of the same old story, but God redeeming that old story into something beautiful and new. This is true not only of the numbers we see in the Bible, but our lives as well.

Discussion Questions:

1. This chapter contained three examples where one story in the Bible reverses or redeems another. Where else in the Bible do we see this take place?

2. How have you experienced God reversing or redeeming your own life or your own story?

3. How might this "pattern of redemption" change how you approach some of the more confusing passages in the Bible?

THE SUM IS GREATER THAN THE PARTS:

COMBINING NUMBERS IN THE BIBLE

"After this I looked, and there before me was a great multitude that no one could count, from every nation, tribe, people and language, standing before the throne and before the Lamb. They were wearing white robes and were holding palm branches in their hands."

– Revelation 7:9, NIV

"Surrounding the throne were twenty-four other thrones, and seated on them were twenty-four elders. They were dressed in white and had crowns of gold on their heads."

– Revelation 4:4, NIV

While in many sports, every score counts as one point (or perhaps two), American football chooses to be different. As a fan, you quickly learn to figure out what combinations of scoring plays lead to a particular score. If your team wins 17-14, you likely assume that both teams scored two touchdowns (seven points each — technically six, but the extra point is almost automatic), but your team was able to kick a field goal. In football, seventeen usually equals two touchdowns and a field goal (17=7+7+3). Are there other ways to reach seventeen? Yes, but watching games and seeing scores trains your mind to see patterns. A score of 28-27 likely means one team scored four touchdowns and the other three touchdowns and two field goals (though it is possible someone missed an extra point).

This is not a book about football, but about the numbers in the Bible. However, the value of pattern recognition is the same in both In football, it is not just the numbers seven and three that matter (the most common scoring plays), but the combinations of sevens and threes that produce a different number. In the Bible, the numbers themselves can have meanings that play out as they are repeated throughout the Biblical story. Yet, sometimes these numbers are combined in ways that draw several meanings together or even enhance the meaning beyond what the number by itself would convey.

In this brief chapter, we will look at three examples of where multiple biblical numbers are added or multiplied together and how that affects their significance in a given biblical passage.

COMPLETE VENGEANCE AND FORGIVENESS: SEVENTY-SEVEN

Combining two numbers in the Bible adds to or enhances their meaning. We have already looked at the redemptive arc of the number seventy-seven in chapter four, but we should take a moment to note that it is the combination of several numbers. Seven, as we have already seen, is a number that represents completeness or perfection. Just as God took seven days to complete creation, things that have seven are seen to be complete or perfect. Seventy is made by multiplying seven and ten together. While ten is often related to worship, law, and judgment, seventy carries the sense of a total number of something. While seven symbolizes completeness in the sense of perfection, seventy means complete in the sense of a full amount or full number.

Thus, combining seven and seventy would communicate a number that is both perfect and that represents the fullness or full amount of something. For Lamech in Genesis 4, seventy-seven-fold vengeance was a way of saying his revenge would be perfect, complete, and full. In Matthew 18, Jesus talks of forgiveness in a way that is also perfect, complete, and full. So far, we are seeing nothing different from what we have already covered in previous chapters.

However, the fact that this is a combined number helps make sense of the difference between different accounts of Jesus' conversation with Peter. In some translations (drawing from some manuscripts), Jesus replies, "I tell you, not seven times, but seventy-seven times" (Mt. 18:22, NIV) — combining seven and seventy by adding them together. However, in other translations, Jesus replies, "I do not say to you, up to seven times, but up to seventy times seven" (Mt. 18:22, NKJV) — combining the same two numbers by multiplication instead of addition.

The same meaning is reached either way, but the different ways of combining the numbers helps us see what is trying to be communicated. Peter asked whether his forgiveness of his brother or sister should be perfect (seven times — Mt. 18:21), but Jesus replies that it must be both perfect and full in number, a much higher number and a much higher bar for forgiveness.

THE MULTITUDE OF GOD'S PEOPLE: 144,000

In two places in the book of Revelation, a number is given of those who are marked and sealed as belonging to the Lord. In Revelation 7, 144,000 are said to be sealed from the tribes of Israel (Rev. 7:4). These have "the seal of the living God" (7:2). Twelve thousand are gathered from each of the tribes of Israel, who are listed by name (7:5-8).[16] Right after Revelation 7 speaks of the 144,000, there is the vision of the great uncountable multitude from every tribe and nation coming before the throne of God (Rev. 7:9). The number 144,000 appears again in Revelation 14, which says:

> Then I looked, and there before me was the Lamb, standing on Mount Zion, and with him 144,000 who had his name and his Father's name written on their foreheads. And I heard a sound from heaven like the roar of rushing waters and like a loud peal of thunder. The sound I heard was like that of harpists playing their harps. And they sang a new song before the throne and before the four living creatures and the elders. No one could learn the song except the 144,000 who had been redeemed from the earth. These are those who did not defile themselves with women, for they remained virgins. They follow the Lamb wherever he goes. They were purchased from

---

[16] It should be noted that the tribe of Dan is left off this list, but that both half-tribes of Joseph (Ephraim, simply called "Joseph" here, and Manasseh) are both listed as contributing 12,000 to the total number.

among mankind and offered as firstfruits to God and the Lamb. No lie was found in their mouths; they are blameless. (Rev. 14:1-5)

Here, the 144,000 are not tied directly to Israel, but to those who belong to the Lamb. They are followers of the Lamb and they sing a new song before his throne. If the first 144,000 are directly tied to Israel and the second 144,000 are the followers of the Lamb, then this gives us clues as to how to understand this number.

There are twelve tribes of Israel and twelve disciples of Jesus. Any reference to twelve in the Bible is going to have some connection with one or both groups. As Revelation 7 (and basic math) makes clear, 144 is reached by multiplying twelve and twelve. In my understanding, 144,000 symbolizes the "full number of disciples" who will be redeemed. By using the same number for both the tribes of Israel sealed to the living God and those marked as belong to the Lamb, this number communicates, I believe, that at the end of all things, God will bring in the fullness of Israel and the fullness of the Gentiles into his kingdom.

I do not believe that 144,000 is intended to be a literal number of those Israelites who will be saved, nor a literal number of those Gentiles who will become disciples of Jesus Christ. As with many of the numbers in Revelation, the intention is symbolic. Twelve times twelve gives us a sense of God bringing in the full harvest of redemption.

24 ELDERS AND 24 THRONES

Twenty-four is a similar combination number as 144, with a similar meaning. 144 is twelve times twelve, but twenty-four is simply twelve plus twelve. In Revelation 4, a door stands open in heaven, and John beholds the throne of God. Then we hear, "Surrounding the throne were twenty-four other thrones, and seated on them were twenty-four elders. They were dressed in white and had crowns of gold on their heads" (Rev. 4:4). There are twelve tribes and twelve disciples. In Matthew 19:28, Jesus promises, "Truly I tell you, at the renewal of all things, when the Son of Man sits on his glorious throne, you who have followed me will also sit on twelve thrones, judging the twelve tribes of Israel" (NIV). However, there are not twelve thrones, but twenty-four around the throne. I think it is likely that this other twelve represents the twelve tribes of Israel, so that the disciples and the tribes share in the worship and judgment around the throne of God.

Like with 144,000, the combination of twelves communicates a drawing together of Jewish and Gentile disciples into the one kingdom of God. The twelve disciples do not replace the twelve tribes (and their elders/patriarchs) around the throne, but join them. In a similar way, the Gentile church does not replace Israel as the people of God, but joins the Israelite church around the throne worshipping the Lamb who was slain.

Conclusion

Seeing how numbers combine in the Bible can be valuable, but we can easily get lost if we dig too deeply. Like the dwarves in Moria, who "delved too greedily and too deep, and disturbed that from which they fled, Durin's Bane,"[17] we can get lost in trying to find secret meaning in the obscure numbers of the Bible and how they combine several other numbers. Combination is the most speculative of the patterns of reading shared in this book and so should carry the least amount of weight in our interpretation. It still

---

[17] J.R.R. Tolkien, *The Fellowship of the Ring* (Ballantine Books: New York, 1965), p. 413)

has value, which is why I have shared it with you, but it should be used cautiously and only in places where a number connects clearly to one of the core biblical numbers (such as seven or twelve).

With that warning, I still find that the principle of combination adds additional layers to my understanding of some particularly challenging biblical numbers, such as the ones shared above. My hope is that, as you grow in reading these numbers, you will find new depths to these passages (without waking up any Balrogs).

Discussion Questions:

1. This chapter claims that the numbers in Revelation are primarily symbolic, not literal. What is your reaction to that claim and why?

2. Pattern recognition helps us read the Bible. How might we develop eyes to see the patterns in the Bible?

Greater Glory:

Comparing Numbers in the Bible

"'The glory of this present house will be greater than the glory of the former house,' says the Lord Almighty."

– Haggai 2:9

"Every exodus in Scripture is incomplete, except the last one"

– Alastair Roberts & Andrew Wilson

Comparison is a natural human activity. Sometimes it is for the better — when, for example, a runner puts up the time of her personal best on the wall as motivation to keep training. Sometimes, though, it is for the worse — when we compare our houses, possessions, or achievements with one another in order to determine who is "better" or "worse." Even in the Bible, there is a place for comparison. When we compare our lives to the standard of God's commandments, we see how far we have fallen short and of our great need for a Savior. Jesus often uses parables to compare common events to the kingdom of God.

Comparison can also be valuable in considering the numbers in the Bible. In this chapter, we will explore what to do when our search for repeated numbers fails to produce any fruit. After getting a handle on the principle of comparison, we will look at two examples that will hopefully help you get a taste of how to do this in your own reading of the Bible.

EXPLANATION OF PRINCIPLE

Our primary principle when reading the Biblical numbers is to ask, "Where else have I seen this number before?" In many circumstances, this will provide myriad connections that will enhance our understanding of a biblical passage. However, sometimes that simply does not work. We do some research and find that the number does not appear anywhere else, or, if it does, it seems totally unconnected and we cannot make heads nor tails of what it might mean. When this happens, it is sometimes valuable to connect passages, not on the basis of number, but on the basis of similar events or circumstances. Then, instead of looking for the same number, we can look at how and why a number is different in different circumstances.

Our normal pattern when we come across a number is to make a connection to another passage based on similar numbers and compare the circumstances, but it is also an important skill to connect passages based on similar circumstances and compare the numbers. Here, we have moved into our third key question to ask for every biblical number:

Question 3: If this number does not repeat, are there other numbers associated with similar events?

Example 1: Temple and Tabernacle Size

Five different times in the Bible, we get a record of almost the same event — God's people constructing the temple or tabernacle. The tabernacle was a mobile tent that travelled with Israel in the wilderness (and after), while the temple was built as a permanent structure for worship of God. However, they are essentially the same building, with the same furnishings, elements, and rooms.

Or are they the same?

Repetition in the Bible is a clue to slow down and pay attention. These five repetitions of the size and construction of the tabernacle/temple should cause us to pause and take a closer look. These accounts are filled with numbers and we can easily get overwhelmed. While there might be value in looking at the significance of the numbers themselves, it is equally (or perhaps *more*) important to consider these numbers in comparison to one another.

For instance, twice in the book of Exodus, we have a record of the dimensions of the tabernacle. Moses receives the blueprint for the tabernacle in Exodus 25-27 and the people build the tabernacle in Exodus 35-40. The same dimensions are recorded in both places (Ex. 26:15-25; Ex. 36:20-30). The Israelites are called to make twenty frames that are a cubit and a half wide and ten cubits tall (Ex. 26:16, 18). That would make the length of the tabernacle 30 cubits (20 x 1.5 = 30). The width of the tabernacle is six frames (Ex. 26:22), or nine cubits (6 x 1.5 =9). There is a lot more detail, but for the sake of illustration, simply remember that the size of the tabernacle was nine cubits by thirty cubits, and it was ten cubits high.

Let's compare that to the record of the temple built by Solomon. In 1 Kings 6, we hear that "The temple that King Solomon built for the Lord was sixty cubits long, twenty wide and thirty high" (v.2). In addition to the temple itself, Solomon built a porch that extended another ten cubits in front of the temple (1 Kings 6:3). Unlike the tent of the tabernacle, a structure was built around the outside of the temple courtyard that was three stories high, with side rooms. Each floor was progressively wider: "The lowest floor was five cubits wide, the middle floor six cubits and the third floor seven" (1 Kings 6:6). The first thing we should notice is that the temple was quite a bit bigger than the tabernacle. The proportions were similar, though not exactly the same (3:1 vs. 10:3), but the temple is twice as long and over twice as wide as the original tabernacle. Size tends to communicate importance. In the ancient world, the greater the god, the greater size the temple should be. The LORD is larger and greater than any temple could hold, since he is the one who created all things. Even the gates of such a large temple as Solomon's were said to need to be lifted up so that God could enter (Ps. 24). Yet, the size of Solomon's temple is meant to communicate something of the grandeur and majesty of God. A big temple for a big God.

When Israel is carted off into exile, having disobeyed God repeatedly, the temple of Solomon is destroyed by the invading Babylonians. The people weep at the destruction of the temple. The entire book of Lamentations is a cry of distress and anguish over the destruction of Jerusalem and the temple. During that period of exile, God gives a vision to the prophet Ezekiel. In that vision (Ezekiel 40-48), Ezekiel is shown a temple area and describes in great detail the dimensions and construction of this temple of the Lord. The dimensions are on a significantly larger scale than even Solomon's temple. The entire compound is five hundred cubits long and five hundred cubits wide (Ezek. 42:15-20).

The inner courtyard is one hundred cubits long and one hundred cubits wide (Ezek. 40:47). Everything in this temple, from the gates to the gatehouses to the kitchens and the altars, is massive in comparison to the descriptions we hear in either Exodus or 1 Kings. For this reason, it has often been associated with the 'heavenly temple' or the true temple of which the earthly temple is but a shadow. A truly immense temple for our great God.

However, when the people return from exile and Zerubbabel begins to rebuild the temple, there are mixed reactions. The altar is built, so that people can perform sacrifices, and the foundation is laid (Ezra 3:1-9). According to the decree of King Darius, the temple mount is expanded to sixty cubits by sixty cubits (Ezra 6:3). This second temple is as long as Solomon's (though shorter if you include Solomon's porch) but significantly wider. However, it is larger than the original tabernacle. The reactions of the people are mixed:

> When the builders laid the foundation of the temple of the Lord, the priests in their vestments and with trumpets, and the Levites (the sons of Asaph) with cymbals, took their places to praise the Lord, as prescribed by David king of Israel. With praise and thanksgiving they sang to the Lord:
> "He is good; his love toward Israel endures forever."
> And all the people gave a great shout of praise to the Lord, because the foundation of the house of the Lord was laid. But many of the older priests and Levites and family heads, who had seen the former temple, wept aloud when they saw the foundation of this temple being laid,

while many others shouted for joy. No one could distinguish the sound of the shouts of joy from the sound of weeping, because the people made so much noise. And the sound was heard far away. (Ezra 3:10-13)

Those who had seen the old temple weep, while those who had never seen a temple rejoice to see what the Lord has provided for them. The prophet Haggai says to the people, "'Who of you is left who saw this house in its former glory? How does it look to you now? Does it not seem to you like nothing?'" (Haggai 2:3). To those who had seen the old temple, this new one seems like nothing. Particularly compared to the glory of the vision given to Ezekiel, this temple falls woefully short. However, the Lord promises through Haggai, "'The glory of this present house will be greater than the glory of the former house,' says the Lord Almighty. 'And in this place I will grant peace,' declares the Lord Almighty." (Haggai 2:9).

In addition to comparing the size of these structures, a similar pattern is seen when we compare the size of the sacrifices at the dedication of these structures. In Numbers 7, there is a list of all the various items offered for the dedication of the tabernacle, with a significant amount of gold and silver for use in the tabernacle itself. However, there are also animal's sacrificed at the dedication:

> "The total number of animals for the burnt offering came to twelve young bulls, twelve rams and twelve male lambs a year old, together with their grain offering. Twelve male goats were used for the sin offering. The total number of animals for the sacrifice of the fellowship offering came to twenty-four oxen, sixty rams, sixty male goats and sixty male

lambs a year old. These were the offerings for the dedication of the altar after it was anointed"(Numbers 7:87-88).

Compare this to the dedication of Solomon's temple, where the numbers are significantly higher: "Solomon offered a sacrifice of fellowship offerings to the Lord: twenty-two thousand cattle and a hundred and twenty thousand sheep and goats. So the king and all the Israelites dedicated the temple of the Lord" (1 Kings 8:63). One of the reasons that the second temple is considered lesser is because it is compared to the temple of Solomon, for consider how much smaller the dedication sacrifice is: "For the dedication of this house of God they offered a hundred bulls, two hundred rams, four hundred male lambs and, as a sin offering for all Israel, twelve male goats, one for each of the tribes of Israel" (Ezra 6:17).

Comparing the size of the structures and the number of sacrifices helps us see more clearly the difference between the tabernacle and temple(s). While there might be value in considering the specific numbers and measurements of the tabernacle and temple, their significance comes into view when we compare the various structures. The tabernacle is a relatively small structure, designed to move along with the people of Israel during their time in the wilderness. The temple of Solomon is a larger, permanent structure that seeks to communicate the glory and grandeur of God. The heavenly temple seen by Ezekiel gives a glimpse of what a truly fitting sanctuary for worshipping the Lord might look like. Though smaller and visually "less" than the temple of Solomon, the second temple will have greater glory. It's glory comes not from its size, but from the fact that the Lord himself will glorify it with his presence.

The comparison of the temple size reminds us that it is

not the size itself that determines how glorious it is, but whether God is present there. This is just as true of churches, church buildings, and ministries as it was with the temple. The size itself is not as significant as whether God is there. Though smaller, the second temple had greater glory: "'The glory of this present house will be greater than the glory of the former house,' says the Lord Almighty. 'And in this place I will grant peace,' declares the Lord Almighty." (Haggai 2:9).

Example 2: Family Size

When God makes his covenant with Abraham, he promises him both land and descendants. Abraham will have a place, a home, where he will live out his calling to be a blessing. He will also have descendants who will be God's people and through his seed all nations will be blessed. The Bible spends a significant amount of space recording the names and numbers of the descendants of Abraham. In part, this is to show God fulfilling his promise to make a nation out of the children of Abraham and that God continues to protect and preserve this people. Yet, the numbers also communicate something else when we compare them. For instance, comparing the number of children in Abraham's family points to a pattern of patience, where God's people are called to patiently wait for God to fulfill his promise. Abraham's brother Nahor has twelve sons (Gen. 22:20-24), but Abraham has two — Ishmael and Isaac[18] — but only one can carry on the covenant — Isaac. Ishmael will have twelve sons (Gen. 25:12-18), but Isaac and Rebekah will struggle with barrenness and have two — Jacob and Esau — but only one

---

[18] Abraham does have other children with his second wife, Keturah (Gen. 25:1-4), but this is only after Isaac has been married and the covenant promise has been passed on to him.

is able to carry on the covenant — Jacob. It is not until the children of Jacob that we see the people begin to multiply as God promised. It takes several generations longer for God's people to experience these blessings than for those out in the world.

Comparison is also helpful in illuminating the significance of the size of the various tribes of Israel. In the book of Numbers, there is a census taken of the people of God. The total number of men aged twenty and older who are available for battle was 603,550 (Num. 1:46). Each of the tribes is listed, but rather than try and do some complicated math to puzzle out some secret meaning from these numbers, we can simply note which tribes are smaller and which tribes are larger. Judah is already the largest by far, with 74,600 members (Num. 1:27), more than the two smallest tribes — Mannasseh and Benjamin — combined (1:34-37). The second-largest tribe, Dan, will face the most tragic fate. Though large at this point, it will not be included in the roster of the people of God in the book of Revelation (Rev. 7:5-8).

At this point, the people of Israel are numerous, but these numbers would dwindle after the exile. The entire number of those who returned from exile from all the tribes is smaller than eight of the tribes' numbers in the wilderness (42,360, cf. Ezra 6:64). Though Israel has broken the covenant and fallen low, God does not abandon them and he does indeed preserve a remnant.

While the comparison of the temple and tabernacle shows God's presence and glory in both large and small structures, the comparison of the size of Israel's tribes reminds us of God's faithfulness. He is faithful in the times where there is growth and visible success (Numbers) and he faithfully keeps us when we stumble, struggle, and fall

(Ezra). Ultimately, he will keep and preserve his people all the way to the end (Rev. 7). What is true for Israel is also true for us as God's people. God is faithful and will guard and keep us when life is blessed, when we fail, and all the way to the end, when we will see him face to face. As Paul says, "What if some were unfaithful? Will their faithlessness nullify the faithfulness of God? By no means!" (Rom. 3:3-4).

Conclusion

This way of reading Scripture is all about finding connections. We can make connections between specific numbers as they are used through the Bible, but we can also make connections between similar circumstances where larger or smaller numbers are used. In addition to the examples in this chapter, we can look at the differences in ages of the patriarchs, the relative ages before and after the flood, or even the number 666 in the book of Revelation. All these are places where comparison yields interesting results.

However, making the connection itself is never enough. We must begin to ask our final question, **"What is God trying to tell us through it?"** Nothing is in the Bible by accident. Slowing down and paying prayerful attention should lead us to wrestle with the purpose for which God included these details. In the final chapter, we will try to put together all of what we have learned by exploring Jesus' two feeding miracles: the feeding of the four thousand and the feeding of the five thousand.

Discussion Questions:

1. How does comparing the numbers relieve some of the pressure to find meaning in every single number?

2. "This way of reading Scripture is all about finding connections." Since starting this book, where have you begun to see connections in your own Bible reading?

3. A bigger temple did not always mean greater glory. How does this impact how you see the "great" things in the world and the "small" things in your own life?

4. God was faithful when Israel's numbers were large and when they were small. How does this impact how you see God's faithfulness in the various seasons of your life?

Loaves, Fish, and Baskets:

The Feeding Miracles as a Case Study for Biblical Numbers

"When Jesus landed and saw a large crowd, he had compassion on them, because they were like sheep without a shepherd."

– Mark 6:34

"If hunger can lead us astray and dehumanize us, so too hunger can draw us back to God and become the starting place for leading a more fully human life."

– Brad Roth

When I first started seriously learning chess, there was a lot of study involved. I not only needed to know how the pieces moved, but I needed to learn openings for white and black, to understand tactics and variations, and to memorize endgame techniques. All of this was very valuable, but eventually I simply needed to play the games. All that study was preparation, but I would only really develop my skills at chess by playing real games against other people. I would sometimes forget what I had learned, I would blunder pieces and make mistakes, but eventually I had to get out of books and onto the board. I needed to translate my theoretical knowledge into "over the board" knowledge.

We have spent six chapters learning methods and approaches for understanding the numbers in the Bible. These "methods" are more like guidelines that I have developed over time by trying to read slowly, deeply, and well. However, we also need to translate our theoretical knowledge of the biblical numbers into "over the board" knowledge. We need to gain practical experience reading the biblical numbers in a way that we look for connections, reversals, combinations, and comparisons. Our knowledge only "works" if it works when we are actually reading the Bible ourselves.

In this last chapter, I want us to examine two similar feeding miracles in the Gospels that contain distinct details (particularly in the numbers involved). By looking at both the feeding of the five thousand (Mt. 14:13-21; Mark 6:30-44; Luke 9:10-17; John 6:1-15) and the feeding of the four thousand (Mt. 15:29-39; Mark 8:1-10), we will hopefully get a better sense of how to apply what we have learned in this book to the reading of various passages in the Bible. As we read, I will pull back the curtain a little on the process and even show you the places where I hit dead ends and had to keep wrestling with the passage. My hope is that you will be encouraged by seeing both the fits and starts, as well as, the final results of trying to read this way.

LOAVES AND FISHES 1: THE FEEDING OF THE FIVE THOUSAND

The feeding of the five thousand is one of only two miracles recorded in all four Gospels. The other is the resurrection of Jesus from the dead. Only Matthew and Mark record both feeding miracles and in both, the feeding of the five thousand takes place first.

Going back all the way to chapter one, we can begin by looking at the immediate context for this event: What is happening right before this story that helps us understand it?

In Matthew, Mark, and Luke, this event takes place right after Jesus has learned about the death of John the Baptist (Mt. 14:1-12; Mk. 6:14-29; Luke 9:7-9). In Matthew and Mark, the event itself is recorded immediately before the miracle (Mt. 14:1-12; Mk. 6:14-29), whereas in Luke, Jesus has only just heard about it (Luke 9:7-9). In John, Jesus has healed someone who was paralyzed for thirty-eight years, before entering into a controversy about his authority to heal on the Sabbath (John 5). In three out of four Gospels, the feeding of the five thousand follows right on the heels of the death of John.

The meal that Jesus sets for five thousand men (not including the women and children, so possibly more than ten thousand people) is set alongside the exclusive banquet of Herod. Herod has a birthday feast for only his high officials and military commanders (Mk. 6:21). He longs to be entertained, and when he is pleased, he ends up taking the life of John as a "gift" for the daughter of Herodias (Mk. 6:22-24). Herod prepares a feast in his palace and takes life, instead of giving it. By contrast, Jesus is filled with compassion (Mk. 6:34). He sees the people hungry and in need. These are not the high and mighty of Herod's court, but the crowds of everyday people who want to see Jesus. When the disciples tell Jesus to send these people away, Jesus responds instead by commanding the disciples to feed them. When the disciples claim they cannot, citing that they only have five loaves and two fish (a young boy's lunch), Jesus takes what is offered and multiplies it to feed thousands. Jesus prepares a feast in the wilderness and instead of taking life, he gives it by feeding the hungry people. The context of this passage already draws the contrast between Jesus and Herod, between the meal and ways of this world, and the meal and way of Jesus.

Where does this take place? It takes place in Galilee, near Bethsaida (Luke 9:10). Jesus goes to a deserted place (Mk 6:31), heads up the mountain (John 6:3), and has the people sit down on the green grass (Mk 6:39). The wilderness, green grass, and the mountain all connect this meal miracle to other passages in the Bible. While the people were in the wilderness, God rained down manna from heaven every day to feed them. God provided food for the hungry — their daily bread. Sitting on "green grass" (Mk. 6:39) is a specific detail that calls to mind Psalm 23 — "The Lord is my shepherd, I lack nothing. He makes me lie down in green pastures, he leads me beside quiet waters" (Ps. 23:1-2). When Jesus feeds the five thousand, he is the Lord providing manna in the desert, he is the Good Shepherd who feeds his lambs. The location, placement within the narrative, and surrounding details all draw this passage into conversation with various feeding miracles in the Bible.

However, what do the numbers in the passage tell us? At the end of the miracle, Jesus feeds five thousand men (not counting the women and children — Mt. 14:21). Five thousand is a fairly rare number in the Bible. It is the weight

LOAVES, FISH, AND BASKETS

of Goliath's armor in shekels (1 Sam. 17:5). It is the amount of men that Joshua used to set an ambush between Bethel and Ai (Joshua 8:12). When the Benjamites are punished for murdering the Levite's concubine, after the Benjaminites are defeated at Gibeah, another five thousand are killed as they flee toward the wilderness (Judges 20:45). When David calls for gifts to be given for the building of Solomon's temple, the leaders of the families give five thousand talents and ten thousand darics of gold (1 Chr. 29:7). Though interesting, none of these other instances of five thousand have obvious connections with this story. However, there are two other times where "five thousand" is used that may shed a bit more light.

In Acts 4, Peter and John are arrested and jailed for preaching about Jesus Christ. Though they are brought before the Sanhedrin for preaching of Jesus' resurrection, "many who heard the message believed; so the number of men who believed grew to about five thousand" (Acts 4:4). The word goes forth and five thousand believe.

Toward the end of 2 Chronicles, King Josiah discovers the book of God's law in the temple. When he reads it, he tears his robes and wants to discover just what he must do, because those who have gone before them have not keep God's word (2 Chr. 34:19-22). In response to the advice of the prophetess Huldah, Josiah renews the covenant and calls upon the entire nation to celebrate the Passover. Josiah, his officials, and the Levites provide sacrificial animals for the families to celebrate the Passover. In this list, we hear, "Also Konaniah along with Shemaiah and Nethanel, his brothers, and Hashabiah, Jeiel and Jozabad, the leaders of the Levites, provided five thousand Passover offerings and five hundred head of cattle for the Levites" (2 Chr. 35:9). When the people are like sheep without a shepherd (as they have been for generations), Josiah steps up to lead them in covenant faithfulness and provides them with food to celebrate the Passover meal. While Josiah's personal generosity is greater (2 Chr. 35:7), some families contribute a total of five thousand offerings for Passover meals.

The repetition of "five thousand" and the presence of a meal point to a connection between these passages, which is strengthened by the fact that the feeding of the five thousand takes place when, "The Jewish Passover Festival was near" (John 6:4). The connection is further strengthened by the language around the meal itself. "Taking the five loaves and the two fish and looking up to heaven, he gave thanks and broke the loaves. Then he gave them to his disciples to distribute to the people. He also divided the two fish among them all" (Mk. 6:41). These words — take, give thanks, broke, gave — are used again at the Passover meal, when Jesus will eat with his disciples and transform and fulfill the meal by proclaiming that it points to his death and resurrection: "While they were eating, Jesus took bread, and when he had given thanks, he broke it and gave it to his disciples, saying, "Take it; this is my body" (Mk. 14:22). Jesus feeding five thousand connects to Josiah and covenant renewal and, together, they connect to the Passover and the Lord's Supper.

Alongside "five thousand," there are other significant numbers in this passage. While there could be important work around the two hundred denarii worth of bread to be bought (Mk. 6:37) or the fact that Jesus has them sit down in groups of hundred and fifties (Mk. 6:40; Lk 9:14), the number of loaves, fish, and leftovers stand out because they are different than what we will see in the later feeding of the four thousand.

When Jesus asks how much supplies they have for the

meal, the disciples reply that they only have five loaves and two fish (Mk. 6:38; Mt. 14:17; Luke 9:13). We might try to find the significance of these numbers by combining them (5+2 = 7), as seven is the number of completeness and parallels the amount of supplies for the later feeding of the four thousand (seven loaves — Mk. 8:5; Mt. 15:34). In this sense, the five loaves and two fish could communicate that, though they have too little in the eyes of the world, what they brought is enough for what Jesus planned to do. Jesus took their full offering and turned it into abundance.

The twelve baskets of leftovers should also make us think of the people of Israel (twelve tribes). When we see the details of the setting (Galilee) alongside the timing (Passover) and the significance of the numbers (5000, 5+2, 12), a picture begins to emerge. In the feeding of the five thousand, Jesus is the one who feeds and shepherds the people of Israel. He sets a banquet for the beloved people of God. They are cared for and welcomed by the Lord Jesus. This miracle of multiplication happens for the hungry of Israel, who are like sheep without a shepherd, and who long to be fed. Jesus not only gives them enough for daily bread (like manna in the wilderness), but an abundance that provides leftovers for the people of God.

This connection to Israel and the Passover also suggests that there may also be wisdom in thinking of the five loaves and two fish separately. Some of the early church fathers suggested that the five loaves may represent the five books of the Law.[19] If so, the Israel connection is only strengthened. They come hungry. All that they have is the

---

[19] For an example of this view, see Augustine, Sermon 80 on the New Testament. The views on the significance of the two fish vary — monarchy and priesthood, love of God and love of neighbor, the two tables of the Law, the two tablets of the Law, the two natures of Christ, the two ways he feeds the church. I am not settled on a particular interpretation. The number two does

Law, but it is enough for Jesus. He takes it and multiplies it to feed the people, with much left over. In some ways, this is a fitting way to read what Jesus is doing in the Sermon on the Mount — he is taking the five loaves of the Law, then blessing and giving them to the people in a way that feeds and nourishes life (Mt. 5-7).

LOAVES AND FISH 2: THE FEEDING OF THE FOUR THOUSAND

Only Matthew and Mark record Jesus performing a second feeding miracle. Most of the details are the same, as well as most of the connections to the Lord's Supper and Jesus providing abundance out of the little that we have to offer. However, the location and the specific numbers referenced point to Jesus feeding, not Israel, but the nations. Thus, in these two miracles, Jesus' blessings and life-giving work go out to both Jew and Gentile.

First, the location. Matthew tells us that this miracle takes place in the desert and that Jesus has the people sit on the ground (instead of grass — Mt. 15:33; 35). However, Mark tells us that this event takes place in the Decapolis (Mk. 7:31 as the setting for Mk. 8:1-9), a Gentile region on the far side of the Sea of Galilee.[20] The Decapolis is filled with people who did not know the Lord and are not in covenant relationship with him. While Jesus performs miracles in the Decapolis (and elsewhere) the majority of his ministry centers in Galilee.

Repetition is a clue to pay attention, and almost the exact same miracle happening twice should force us to

---

not have a clear enough central meaning in the Bible that I feel comfortable giving a confident answer.

[20] It is possible that the Decapolis was what Jesus' original hearers would have imagined "the far country" to be in the Parable of the Prodigal Son (Luke 15:13).

pause. Why did Jesus do the same thing again? Was it just that there was another hungry crowd or is there something deeper going on?

The most significant difference between the two feeding miracles is that when Jesus feeds the five thousand, he is feeding Jews, but when he feeds the four thousand, he is feeding Gentiles. Both crowds are hungry (physically and spiritually), both receive compassion from Jesus (Mt. 14:14; Mk. 8:2), and both are nourished by Jesus. These acts of feeding both Jews and Gentiles underscore the promise of the kingdom of God, that it will be one people formed from every tribe and nation (Rev. 7:9).

What about the numbers? I had hoped that there would be as many significant insights from the number four thousand as there were from five thousand, but four thousand is an even rarer number. It only occurs in four other places in the Bible. In 1 Samuel, Israel loses a battle with the Philistines and four thousand people die (1 Sam. 4:2). Both 1 Kings and 2 Chronicles record that King Solomon has four thousand stalls for his chariots (1 Kings 4:26; 2 Chr. 9:25). Chariots were the height of military technology and often seen as symbolic of worldly power (Ps. 20:7; Is. 31:1), but there is nothing in this feeding miracle to suggest the Gentile connection has anything to do with power. In 1 Chronicles, the list of Levites serving in the temple includes four thousand serving as gatekeepers and four thousand praising with musical instruments (1 Chr. 23:5). Again, no connection jumps out at me. Is the number supposed to be a comparison, since Jesus feeds five thousand Jews but only four thousand Gentiles? There is nowhere in the Bible that seems to suggest that there will be less Gentiles in the church than Jews (rather, quite the opposite).

The seven loaves and seven leftover baskets seem a bit more promising for understanding the numerical significance. Seven is the number of completeness, but also creation. Jesus feeds not only his people (the five thousand), but all of the world (the four thousand). Though it would have seemed little in the eyes of the world, what they offer (seven loaves) is enough — a complete offering. Jesus multiplies it so that the people not only eat, but there is a full amount left over. At the end of the feast, there are not just a few crumbs, but seven baskets full.

In this way, the numbers of loaves and leftovers communicate similar meanings to the five loaves, two fish, and twelve baskets in the feeding of the five thousand, but without the references to Israel. This seems fitting, since the major difference between the two miracles is not their size, but the recipients of the miracle.

How to make sense of it?

Learning to read the Biblical numbers is more art than science. As I demonstrated in this case study, sometimes looking for these connections yields very interesting and surprising results. We saw a new connection between Jesus feeding the five thousand and Josiah's work of covenant renewal and revival of the Passover. We saw how the loaves and baskets highlighted that Jesus is feeding and nourishing Israel, which only strengthened themes seen throughout the passage. However, we also saw that not every investigation gives clear answers. I could not find any significance to the fact that Jesus feeds four thousand instead of five thousand in the second miracle. Perhaps it is different only to set it apart as a distinct miracle. There are even those who think this is the same miracle recorded twice, but the different details indicate these are separate events.

While diving into the biblical numbers yielded mixed results, the process of slowing down and paying attention to these kind of details helps bring the miracles into focus. We see Jesus as the Good Shepherd who feeds his lambs and as the Lord who provides manna in the wilderness and sets a table for his people at the Passover. We also see the depth and width of the mission of Jesus. Jesus takes the Law and multiplies and shares it in a way that it gives life to his people. Jesus feeds not only those of the people of Israel, but those of the Decapolis — those of the nations — as well. Already in the Gospels, the life-giving work of Jesus reaches out to the lost of the world, who are hungry and in need of compassion.

Conclusion

Eventually, we need to get out of the books and into *the* book, the Bible. We need to bring together all that we have learned by reading and studying passages of the Bible. While the numbers in the Bible should not generally bear the whole weight of our understanding of a passage, they often fill out the meaning communicated by other details.

The two feeding miracles in the Gospels serve as a test case for the benefits and limitations of reading the biblical numbers. The process of reading the biblical numbers is really an extension of the understanding of how to read the Bible that we explored back in chapter 1. When we believe that all Scripture is God-breathed, that no detail is there by accident, that God is the ultimate author of Scripture, and that the Spirit inspired and guided the writing, composition, and preservation of the Bible, we can begin to look for connections across the Bible, because we expect God to be saying the same thing in different places and in different ways. This slower and broader reading of the Bible is not inventing connections where there are none, but uncovering connections that already exist.

Discussion Questions:

1. Not every number we looked at in this chapter gave a clear meaning. Did you find that encouraging or discouraging? Why?

2. Does this case study give you more or less confidence that you could try to read this way yourself? What tools might you need to be able to read this way?

3. How might you practice "slowing down and paying attention to the details" when reading the Bible?

4. What did you hear about the feeding miracles of Jesus in this chapter that you had never considered before?

Conclusion

"They asked each other, 'Were not our hearts burning within us while he talked with us on the road and opened the Scriptures to us?'"

– Luke 24:32

I love sharing insights from the Bible. The dinner and evening conversations in our home are frequently peppered with, "Did you ever think about…" or "If I told you this happened in the Bible, could you tell me what story I am in?" (hint: the point is that there is always more than one story). This book was born out of that passion to see people approach the Bible with joy and wonder rather than fear and anxiety. The Bible was written over centuries by multiple authors in cultures vastly different than the one I experience in North America. This makes parts of the Bible more challenging for me to understand.

But instead of shaking our heads in confusion, skipping over a passage, or shrugging our shoulders and thinking, "this must be something only the experts can understand," our goal has been to equip everyday Christians to lean into the challenging sections of the Bible.

This book focuses on the numbers in the Bible because they are one place where I used to stumble. However, because I consciously slowed down and looked for connections, the numbers have become something exciting to encounter when I read the Bible. My hope is that this book has helped awaken some of that excitement in you as well.

How far have we come?

As we close this book, let's pause and realize just how far we have come in learning how to read the numbers in the Bible. In chapter 1, we said that we need to understand what the Bible is and what it is for before we can begin to ask how to read it. We looked at some key characteristics of the Bible, its purpose in the church and for discipleship, and the basic approach to reading the Bible — whole-part-whole.

In chapter 2, we unveiled the four key questions that we should ask whenever we encounter a number in the Bible: "Where else does this number appear in the Bible?", "Does this instance continue or reverse the themes found in the other instances of this number?", "If this number does not repeat, are there other numbers associated with similar events?", and "Why was this number included in this passage?"

Chapter 3 focused on the first question by looking at repeated numbers, such as seven and twelve, and by asking ourselves where we should look to find their central meaning.

Chapter 4 explored a different kind of repetition. Some numbers repeat and, in doing so, repeat the same theme. However, other numbers show a pattern of redemption throughout the Bible.

Chapter 5 briefly explored numbers that are a combination of two other biblical numbers and how to combine the meanings as we combine the numbers.

Chapter 6 looked at what to do when a number doesn't repeat. In these cases, it can be helpful to look for repeated events or circumstances and ask why one number would be greater or less in a similar circumstance at a different time or place. We paid particular attention to the size of the temple and the size of the tribes of Israel, which are very different in different times in the Bible.

In chapter 7, we attempted to put all of these methods to use by reading through the two feeding miracles in the Gospels — the feeding of the five thousand and the feeding of the four thousand. We got a live and unfiltered look at the process of examining numbers and how it sometimes leads to dead ends, but usually produces some fruit.

We have come a long way in a fairly short book. However, the journey is just beginning. Let me end with one piece of advice as you seek to grow in this process of reading the Bible well.

PRACTICE MAKES PROGRESS, NOT PERFECT

When I was a child, I learned the phrase, "Practice makes perfect." It was meant to be an encouragement to practice and to remind you that you will not do it perfectly the first time you try. However, my children have learned a better phrase at school, "Practice makes progress, not perfect." They recognize that they will never be finished learning, never be perfect, but that "perfection" is not the goal of learning. The goal is progress. The goal is to learn and practice and be a little better today than you were yesterday. This is especially true when reading the Bible. We will never reach perfection, but we can always continue to grow. That growth comes through practice, through daily reading and stumbling and sometimes joyous discovery.

As we saw in examining the feeding of the four thousand, not every number has a clearly defined symbolic meaning. At least, not every number has one that I have discerned *so far*. I am still practicing and making progress. After this book is published, as I keep on reading the Bible, there may be new discoveries that I would have loved to include in this book. But if I had waited to share my discoveries with you until I understood them all, this book would never have been written.

In Genesis 15, God tells Abraham to "Look up at the sky and count the stars—if indeed you can count them."(Gen. 15:5). The number of the stars would be the number of Abraham's descendants. If it was possible for Abraham to count all the stars in the sky, then it would be possible for him to count all the people who would belong to the covenant he had with the Lord. This is an incredible promise from God. However, "counting the stars" was something Abraham could never finish. The point wasn't to get an accurate measurement so that he could quantify his descendants. The point was to look at the sky and see a visual representation of the good promises of God.

You don't need to be perfect in understanding the biblical numbers (or any aspect of Scripture). You won't be. However, my encouragement is to keep reading, keep practicing, keep patiently trusting that God put all of this here in the Bible for a reason. Like Abraham counting the stars, we will never reach an ending to reading the Bible. That is not the point. Instead, we should look and see the good promises of God. And if the work of reading doesn't yield clear results today, then give thanks to God today and come back tomorrow.

For reading Scripture well is the work and joy of a lifetime.

Acknowledgements

No book reaches publication on its own. I want to offer special thanks to my father and editor, Tim Shaffer, who did extensive proofreading on this book. Any mistakes that remain are surely my own, but the book is better for your having worked on it.

For Bethel Reformed Church, thank you for reading and studying the Bible with me these past years. Thank you for bearing witness to the breadth and depth of the mercy of Jesus.

For Olga, thank you for all that you do to make books like this possible. I cannot name the number of roles you filled in this process. You were a mother, wife, cover designer, proofreader, beta-reader, typesetter, and sounding board – just to name a few. You put up with my crazy writing habits and unrealistic deadlines with grace and patience. Thank you for being my partner in these projects and in the wonderful adventure of our family.

For Elijah, Moriah, and Joanna, thank you for loving Jesus, asking excellent questions, and loving your Daddy as he writes books. You are always in my heart and on my mind as I write.

Also by
Stephen C. Shaffer

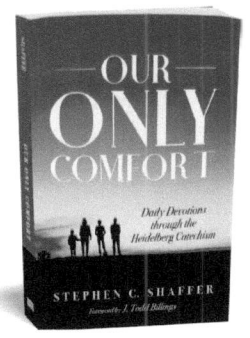

Our Only Comfort:
Daily Devotions through the Heidelberg Catechism

In a fast-paced world full of distractions, how do we create space to have conversations about faith? Parents long to talk about Jesus with their children, but are unsure where to begin. Families want to slow down and reconnect with what matters most, but struggle to squeeze anything into already busy schedules. Teens and adults desire to go deeper in their faith, but are filled with unanswered questions. In *Our Only Comfort*, Rev. Stephen Shaffer provides individuals and families with a helpful structure for growing in Christian faith. In a series of 364 devotions, *Our Only Comfort* will take families, young adults, and new believers through the core teachings of the Christian faith through the lens of the Heidelberg Catechism. Wrestling through questions like "Who is Jesus?" "How do I pray?" and "What does it mean to keep the Ten Commandments?" these short devotions create opportunity for conversations about faith between parents and children and provide nourishment for faith to grow.

Paperback: 978-1725298736
Hardcover: 978-1725298743

All Things Hold Together:
Recovering Christian Worldview

In Christ, all things hold together. Apart from him, things fall apart. The multitude of fractures in our world result from the removal of our center in Christ. Worldview is not a weapon. It was meant to mend the fractures opened up by the modern world. The recovery of a theological center, of a Christian worldview, serves as a way to sew back together what the modern world seeks to rip apart. Worldview gives voice to a way before and beyond the fractures, a world we have abandoned in order to rule ourselves.

Paperback: 978-1777978761
Hardcover: 978-1777978754

Rooted: Growing in Christ in a Rootless Age

In a rootless world, we long for a place where we find peace, rest, and belonging.

The soil of our society is not particularly well-suited for growing deep roots of character and Christian identity. The consistent pattern of uprooting our lives and families for a new job, a new opportunity, a new church has left our roots damaged, our friendships weak, and our souls drained. We long for a place where we are known, loved, and even challenged to live more fully.

The longing for home, for place, for rootedness is ultimately a longing for Jesus. Wrestling with the biblical themes of land and exile, *Rooted: Growing in Christ in a Rootless Age* is a call to grow more at home in our true home, Jesus Christ. Walking along with Israel from Eden through the Exodus to the Exile, Stephen C. Shaffer shows how God both rooted and uprooted his people so that they would find their identity and center in God.

Paperback: 978-1777978709
Hardcover: 978-1777978716

The Sinews of Scripture: A Handbook on Biblical Genealogies

Biblical genealogies do not have to be intimidating.

For many people, coming across a list of unfamiliar names in the Bible serves as a stumbling block. We know it should be important, but are unclear how to make sense of it. In The Sinews of Scripture, Stephen Shaffer demystifies the genealogies of the Bible and provides tools to read the whole Bible well. With chapters on the purpose of genealogies, how to read the Bible, and an exploration of eight different biblical genealogies, this book contains a wealth of information and practical advice for the everyday Bible reader. Drawing from years of preaching and teaching the genealogies, Stephen Shaffer will make the genealogies come alive and show how they draw the various parts of Scripture together and point us to Jesus.

Paperback: 978-1777978792

www.ingramcontent.com/pod-product-compliance
Ingram Content Group UK Ltd.
Pitfield, Milton Keynes, MK11 3LW, UK
UKHW042003230426
12048UKWH00009B/527